The Cricketer

A Story based on an Ancient Fable of

'The Hindu Ball God'

by
Ian Feldman

SSI Publishing, LLC
P.O. Box 815
Holly Springs, GA 30142
USA

Copyright 2024 © Ian Feldman

Table of Contents

PART ONE: THE SWAT VALLEY

PART TWO: COSCO STADIUM

PART ONE

THE SWAT VALLEY

Chapter 1

The Private Island

We begin on a 'Private Island', hidden somewhere in the Southern Hemisphere of the Indian Ocean, off the West Coast of Australia. It's their 'Winter' of the Year '2038'...

The aqua blue waters of this great ocean, lap the white sandy beaches of a remote tropical paradise. Tall graceful palm trees move ever so slightly in a gentle sea breeze, as we spy a large opulent mansion set back, from the beach.

The cleared area around the mansion seems largely abandoned other than a few painted storks fishing at a brackish lagoon's edge, while a pair of green Alexandrine parrots call out as they flutter from a domed dragon blood tree.

Brightly colored lizards are scampering about in the presence of a dozen 'Black-Uniformed Security Guards' patrolling the area, some on foot and others driving quietly around in camouflaged off-road four-wheelers.

At a nearby resort styled swimming pool, a handsome young well-groomed and tanned twenty something man, sits alone in the lavish surroundings. He's relaxing on the end of the swimming pool's diving board, as he suddenly stares directly into our camera-like view.

"I'm Raji Swat and my entire 'Life' has been a complete cycle of continuous 'Fortuitous Events'.

I am now twenty-two years old, born on a leap-year in 2016, in the Swat Valley which lies below the Himalayan Mountains in Pakistan. It is often called 'the Switzerland' of Asia, except for one thing.

It's a poor area that 'most' who are born there, 'never escape'."

Raji gestures around to his opulent surroundings.

"As you can see, however, I have escaped from the poverty of my people in the Swat, to enjoy an affluent and elegant lifestyle on my own 'isolated' private island."

Raji gazes off into the distance for a moment, then faces back into view again.

"Ironically though, I miss the 'Swat' every day of my life."

A bittersweet smile envelops Raji's face.

"Look at me!"

Raji stands abruptly on the end of the diving board. Although the board is narrow, Raji does not falter. His legs are strong and his balance is perfect.

"I am a small-framed young man. I do not seem to be particularly strong or athletic."

Raji plops back down, again sitting on the board which bounces slightly up and down for a moment.

"You will be surprised to learn that I am one of the wealthiest sports stars that the world has ever known.

I do not boast, but only tell you what is 'truth'. I am worth literally billions of American dollars in earnings and endorsements from my sports career. . .

And just remember, I'm only twenty-two and have many years ahead of me to make billions more."

Raji stands, then quickly dives into the alluring crystal waters of the luxurious infinity pool. He surfaces, pushes his wet black hair back and looks into the 'camera-like' view again.

"You may ask, why I am here, living in this exquisite mansion on this remote island and isolated from the world. . . and not back in the 'Swat Valley'. . . my home and where those, I have known and love, reside.

Then, let me take you back into my 'Life' so you may see for yourself my reasons. . ."

SUDDENLY, we are drawn though time, to an exclusive RESTAURANT somewhere, late night.

Raji exits the posh restaurant and is deluged by throngs of FANS who push and elbow their way to reach out to him.

Several sports groupies rush in and pull strands of his hair; others grasp at his clothing, ripping and tearing at it; still others lunge at him and nearly knock him to the ground.

Three BODYGUARDS rescue him and spirit him away, disappointing his ardent fans. As he is escorted off, Raji looks back at the mob, disheartened and dismayed.

"What you've observed is 'My Simple Truth'. The zealotry of fans who unrelentingly pursue me. This is what has chased me to this hideaway.

The 'yin and yang' of my new life is in full play. My phenomenal success is tempered by those who will not allow me to live in 'True Freedom'. A life of peaceful existence."

Raji swims to the side of the pool and pulls himself out. He drapes a towel around his waist and heads for the mansion. He glances once more at us, as he walks off.

"Just how I became one of the biggest success stories in the world of sports is something of a mystery, that will surprise you.

Not that it can be replicated because it is a unique path, that I would wish, for no one. And I hope, no one else will ever be forced to follow.

So allow me to tell you a story which runs the gamut from the 'magical to the horrid', from 'violence and prejudice to justice and destiny', from 'squalid struggles and poverty', to a 'sports hero and legend' with untold wealth and fame.

It is a legacy that has made me what I am today."

SWAT VALLEY – PAKISTAN:

We begin. . . 'Twelve years before 2038'. . .

The beautiful snow covered and bleak Himalayan Mountains are the backdrop of this arid, blighted valley that is nearly bereft of plant life, but alive with small dirt devils stirred up by an eerie wind that whistles through it.

A group of Muslim women covered head to toe in their jilbab Islamic garb, walk through the area, their small children running ahead of them and playing games of imagination.

At once, Raji softly begins our perspective of his early life. . .

"As a Hindu child, it was difficult growing up in the Swat since the Islamic religion was predominant."

Raji, then only ten years old, runs out of a rustic school past the Muslim women and their children, carrying a decrepit 'cricket bat' over his shoulder.

A Muslim boy of seven years, spots Raji, picks up a rock and throws it at him, striking him on the shoulder. Raji grabs, his unprovoked malicious wound, pulls his hand back and sees that it's covered in blood.

"There was very little tolerance for the 'Hindus or Buddhists' in this part of Pakistan where 'hate' for us was taught in Mosques. Our only haven was the old 'British Mission School', we attended."

THE HIGH MOUNTAINS – North of the Swat Valley. . .

Undetected by the villagers, a group of 'Taliban Terrorists' descend a well-traveled mountain path, armed with Chinese AK-74 assault rifles, PK machine guns, semiautomatic pistols and large very sharp sabres. They are wearing traditional Taliban garb and white turbans. Each terrorist has extra ammunition in bandoliers crisscrossed over their chests.

Raji continues, softly defining an event. . .

"Worse than the general shunning and harassment that I and my Hindu friends experienced in the 'Swat', was the raids by the Taliban Terrorists. They would frequently come down from their mountains hideaways to raid and plunder the local villages.

On this day the alarms began ringing throughout our village. . .
My mother, Veena, grabbed me, my two sisters and my brother, then hid us in a dilapidated shed away from our house.

The alarms that sounded in the village, warning of this raid were the only hope we had.

Often my mother would hide us in various places to keep the Terrorists guessing. . . but others were not so lucky, as the Taliban terrorists captured young Hindu girls, dragging them away crying and pleading with them.
While other terrorists in their raiding party would set fire to the thatched roofs of our neighbors more fragile huts."

THE BUDDHIST SHRINE:

"When the brutal terrorists saw it unguarded, they entered the village's Buddhist shrine. Then facing a huge stone statue of the Sitting Buddha, one of the terrorists riddled the statue with bullets, while two of his Comrades pushed on it with all their strength and sent it crashing to the floor. The only recognizable remnant of the statue was part of Buddha's peaceful face.

Their objective was to seek out and destroy any symbol or icon that they perceived to be averse to their Islamic beliefs.

Despite the horrors brought upon our village by the Taliban, oddly I was never afraid. I knew deep down inside, that I was destined for greater things. I merely had to survive my childhood."

OUR HINDU TEMPLE:

"On the day of that particular raid, the Taliban terrorists, also burst into our Hindu Temple, shooting and killing several worshipers. They walked up to the altar vandalizing the statues of the Hindu gods that were decorated in precious metals and gems. One of them knocked a statue over onto the floor, then raised his sabre and swiftly severed the statue's head. . .
He then carried out the head of the statue while yelling 'Allahu Akbar', as his comrades dragged out the torso. . . then precious metals and bags of gems were removed, ensuring that they profited from the desecration of Our Shrine."

SWAT VALLEY – LATE NIGHT:

Following that raid, Raji stands alone in the now deserted and desecrated little village of his beloved 'Swat Valley'. His face is stoic as he looks up at the wondrous night sky filled with stars, that look like low-hanging diamonds, carelessly strewn across the galaxy.

"Living in the 'Swat' was more than a challenge. My younger brother and my youngest sister died there . . .which left my mother a broken woman, my oldest sister alone and me with a broken heart forever. . .
Why I miss it escapes all logic.

But perhaps it prepared me for the many challenges that I would one day face in another time and another place. A world, in so many ways, far removed from the ancient 'Valley' of my birth."

THE CRICKET FIELD:

At a small primitive Cricket playing field, ten-year-old Raji and several other local boys are competing aggressively...
Raji pitches the ball to a waiting batter. His throw is fast and accurate... the batter swings and misses, as the ball once again smashes the wickets. Another batter walks away with slumped shoulders, defeated.

The next batter is up. Raji's dynamic pitch eludes the bat of another opponent.

On the sidelines is retired Sergeant Major Anwar Kahmal, sixty years on, who keeps an intense focus on the play. Kahmal shouts out instructions to the boys, animated and intense as he walks up and down the sidelines.

He's yelling at the them, gesturing and motioning play actions, with his massive left hand.

Raji again focuses on his story...

"Retired Major Anwar Kahmal, a teacher at my school, was our coach. I learned the game of 'Cricket' from him. He was my inspiration.

Having been a soldier in the 'British Occupation Army' of Pakistan, a fighting spirit had become the very nature of his being, even in retirement.

In my youth, I absolutely believe that he passed that spirit on to me, and I must attribute much of my later success, to him as well."

LATER – AFTER THE GAME:

"I remember, the boys packing up their gear as they began running off to their homes. Then passing by the Coach, I bowed quickly to Kahmal and started to walk on.
But Kahmal turned toward me commenting . . ."

"Raji! Please a moment for me, my young bowler. . ."

Of course I stopped and ran over to him. . .

"Yes, sir. . ."

Kahmal bent down closer to me, speaking softly, as if to reveal a secret between us. . .

"Just want to tell you, how impressed I am with your play, Raji."

"Thank you, Major. I learned it all from you, Sir."

"Ah, but the talent you displayed today, you were born with. I had nothing to do with that. . .

All I ever hoped to do is channel your talent into positive results. It seems as though I have been successful. . .

You are a special young boy, a 'Natural'."

"Sir, I am not sure what it is to be a natural."

"Sports play comes easy to you, Raji. . .
You are 'naturally a good athlete', even without training."

I smiled at him, wondering where this might take me. . .

"My dream is to become a 'Professional Cricket Player'. Do you think I have a chance, Major?"

It was then that he said it. The 'thing' that we would NEVER mention. . .

"Your 'right arm' is what mine use to be."

Shocked, I furtively glanced at the Major's missing 'right arm', then at once, I looked away.

"Ask me, Raji."

"Sir?"

"My arm is missing. I'm sure you and all the boys are curious. . .
I lost it in the most vicious battle of my military career."

"But you survived, Sir. You must have defeated your enemy."

"True! But I fear that enemy 'lives on' to fight another War. A coming 'War' with a new, more-able opponent from the West. . .

But let's get back to happier thoughts. . .
I am quite positive, that your dream of becoming a 'Cricketer' only awaits your grasping it, Raji."

And to this day, those thoughts he spoke and that moment, stuck in my mind, forever. . .

Chapter 2

The Moment of Transition

We transition in time, to the instant 'Raji's Story' becomes the 'Reality of the Legend', from this moment forward. . .

It's mid-afternoon near Raji's Village, deep in the Swat Valley of Pakistan. . .

Raji is walking with his friend, nine-year old, Adarsh, another Hindu boy. . .

They have set up three wickets to create an impromptu cricket playing field with a bounce board behind the wickets. Using a mud-yellow cricket ball. . . an old British relic, a beaten-up full-sized leather 'team ball', they bat it around.

Raji and Adarsh take turns bowling and batting the ball using several old worn cricket bats. . .

But just as Raji is about to pitch the ball, once again to Adarsh, the 'Village Alarms' start sounding.
Raji screams out to Adarsh. . .

"The Taliban!"

Suddenly, other Village boys who were playing nearby on the field, take off running at full speed to their various hiding places.

Adarsh yells back to Raji, with fear in his voice.

"We must flee. We must run with the others!"

"No . . . We do not run. We stay, Adarsh."

"Are you crazy, Raji?!"

Raji grabs the 'ancient cricket ball' with one hand and Adarsh's hand with the other. He pulls the reluctant Adarsh into an entrance of the nearby 'Hindu Temple' ruins. . .

Raji, entering the ruins, at once is astounded by the hundreds of 'Avatars of Hindu Gods', that line the walls.

Raji is frozen for a moment, amazed as he focuses on the 'mystical avatars'. He is wide-eyed as some of 'their eyes' seem to turn and focus on him alone.

Terrified and frightened, Adarsh angrily pulls his hand free from Raji's grasp as he whispers.

"Raji! Quick. . . we must hide!"

Raji turns and looks at Adarsh, confused. . . The 'spell' broken.

He quickly returns to the reality of the moment and follows Adarsh to a half-wall, where they secrete themselves crouching down and huddling close together.

As Raji peeks around the edge of the wall, his attention is once again drawn back to the Avatars. . .

"These 'Hindu Gods'. I... I feel a connection."

"You, who 'never attends worship' and rejects his own Mother's religion?"

"I cannot explain it, Adarsh."

Raji stands and begins to walk toward the 'Avatars'.

Adarsh's eyes grow wide, in apprehensive fear. Again he whispers softly. . .

"Raji, Raji stay with me! I'm afraid. The terrorists could ambush us at any moment!"

"I... feel safe. I feel the protection of the 'Avatars' here."

"I prefer the protection of this wall. I'll stay put, while you go on your suicide march, Raji."

Raji ignores Adarsh and slowly plods forward to the front of a long line of 'Avatars'. He stops at one that 'seems to return' his gaze.

Raji brushes off the decades of dust from the eroding stone that covers the identity of the Avatar.

He peers closely at the worn-away 'Hindu' lettering. . . as quietly he reads it to himself.

"Hanuman, 'The Right Hand of Rama', Hindu God of Strength and Sport."

Raji looks up at the Avatar's face. The 'Avatar's Eyes' seems to be looking directly at the 'battered old cricket ball' that Raji holds in one hand. He slowly raises his hand bringing the ball closer to the Avatar.

Suddenly, there is the sound of the approaching 'Taliban Terrorists' who are smashing the boys' wickets and slamming their bats just outside the 'Ruins'.
Raji's head snaps toward the 'Entrance' of the ruin, anticipating an ambush. . .

As the 'Lead Terrorist' shouts out before he enters. . .

"ALLAHU AKBAR! ALLAHU AKBAR!"

Raji glances at the 'Hanuman Avatar' once again, then dashes to the wall where Adarsh is hiding.

Adarsh is trembling. Raji grabs Adarsh's hand to calm him.

Then places his hand over Adarsh's mouth so that he does not call out and reveal their location.

Raji peeks around the wall edge once again. He is astounded. The 'Avatar' seems to have literally moved a few inches from the wall!
Hanuman's 'Eyes' are turned, now looking directly at Raji.

Raji stands-up, almost trance-like and hypnotized, as the sandy stone 'Eyes of the Avatar', transform into a 'brilliant red'.
Raji grasps Adarsh's hand with his left hand and pulls him upward. Adarsh struggles to free himself speaking angrily, but in a seething whisper. . .

"Have you gone mad, Raji?! We must stay in hiding."

Raji does not respond. . . with a firm grip he jerks Adarsh along with him and walks toward Hanuman.

As Raji, with the 'old cricket ball' firmly gripped in his right hand, nears the Avatar, the 'glowing red' of his 'Eyes' transforms into a pleasant 'neon blue'. . . drawing Raji even closer to 'Hanuman'.

And, as he slowly approaches, with the 'Avatar's Eyes' tracing his movements . . . he somehow instinctively guides Adarsh behind a limestone column. . . whispering. . .

"We'll be safer here, Adarsh."

Suddenly, four heavily armed Taliban Terrorists burst into the room, rushing directly to the far wall lined with the 'Avatars of the Hindu Gods'. Tears brim in Raji's eyes, as he watches the terrorists, using the boy's own 'Cricket Bats', viciously smash and destroy the Avatars, one by one.

As the terrorists move down the line, closer and closer to 'Hanuman', Raji finally stands up in defiance.
A look of 'rage and determination' encompasses his face. He stands and plants himself defiantly on the ground, holding the 'old cricket ball'.

Raji's hands begin to tremble, when. . .
A 'bright-white electrical volt' races through his entire body. . . sparks of its rapid passage visible to the naked eye. . . the energy of which aggregates in his two hands in a 'dazzling glow'. Raji clings to the 'Cricket Ball' tightly. . .

Then takes a few steps forward. . .as Adarsh tries to spit words into the air. . .

"Raji! Don't leave me!"

Raji turns and again squeezes Adarsh's hand with his left grip. . .as he replies softly

"I must go."

Raji releases Adarsh's hand, then looks at 'Hanuman' whose Eyes have transformed back into their 'glowing red hue'. A hot laser-like beam seems to emanate from 'Hanuman's Fiery Red Eyes'.

At first Raji looks away from the beam and shields himself from its heat and brilliance, but his mind and immortal soul are slowly drawn back to it.

After a few moments, Raji's head falls back and his eyes close, as a general weakness overcomes his body as though he is succumbing to the power of the bright beam into his eyes, into his brain, and ultimately into his soul.

His shoulders slump, his knees are weak and he nearly falters, but suddenly everything becomes clear.

His 'Eyes' snap wide open. He stands erect, 'Stronger', a new resolve in his facial expression, an 'un-earthly-like power' has overtaken him. . .

Raji steps out from behind the column where he was hiding and directly confronts the 'Terrorists', just as one of the them lifts a Cricket Bat, ready to smash 'Hanuman'.

A Deep almost 'evil-like voice' ejects in a scream from Raji's throat!

"RUKANA! . . . STOP!"

Raji grips his ball so tightly, with a power and strength so incredible that the 'leather cricket ball' is crushed and transforms into a 'rock-solid' like object.
Raji winds up and launches the now 'Surreal Object' at 'lightening-speed' hitting the terrorist directly in the center of his forehead.
The impact splits his forehead and instantly smashes the terrorist to the ground, before he even has time to moan in pain.

Raji's eyes are wide with amazement, as the 'Rock-Like Object' with wisps of smoke encircling it, reverses and speeds back toward him, landing painlessly in his right hand, 'ready to launch again'.

Raji repeats the throw of the 'Surreal Rock-Hard Object' once again, at the next terrorist. . .

The man, upon seeing the dead body of his comrade, advances toward Raji. The same fate awaits him as well. Then again, Raji winds up, throws the 'Surreal Rock-Hard Object' like a bullet, and right on target, hits another terrorist's forehead and splits it in two.

The 'Surreal Object' again returns perfectly to Raji, who faces a final terrorist. Raji winds up and strikes him on the exact same spot above his eyes, which splits his head and kills him instantly.

Seeing all this 'fantastical killing' of the vial Terrorists, Adarsh stands and emerges from behind the column, smiling in amazement yelling out to Raji.

"Raji! You have the strength of the 'Mystics'! It's the connection you felt with the 'Hindu Gods'.

I 'Must Run' and tell all the Villagers of this 'Miracle'. How the Gods and Your Power has saved us!"

But Raji starts screaming after Adarsh. . .

"No... No, Adarsh stay here in hiding!
It's still Not Safe out there!"

But in his fervor, Adarsh doesn't listen and keeps running.

In moments, Raji hears the report of automatic gunfire, just outside the 'Ruins Entrance'.

Raji, overcome with panic and anger, carefully crosses to the entrance, peeks around the wall's edge and sees the dead, bullet-ridden body of his friend, Adarsh.
Tears of sadness, then intense rage, well up in Raji's eyes. . .
Once again, his face is contorted in a hypnotic image of pain, grief and ultimately hate. . .

Waiting to react, Raji hears the muffled voices of approaching terrorists.

He rushes across the room to stand beside 'Hanuman' and position himself to face the next onslaught of murderous terrorists.

Two more terrorists enter the 'Ruins'.
Aghast, they look at the split heads and blood of their several dead comrades, and then at 'Raji', the Hindu boy holding a curious rock. They then focus on the 'Fiery Red Eyes' lasering out at them, from the Stone Avatar 'Hanuman', beside the boy.
Rapidly they exchange quick glances with one another. . . shrieking!

"Demon! - Hindu Demon! Run Comrade!"

Stumbling back a few steps in absolute fear, the Terrorists, then turn and run for their lives.

As Raji realizes the carnage he's created and then looks at the 'smoldering rock' that once more returned to his hand, as it transforms back into a 'Leather Cricket Ball'. . .his mind starts spinning. . .
He stares yet again at 'Hanuman' whose eyes are now blank and return to smooth sandstone.

In a trance, Raji slowly walks out of the ruins carrying the 'old leather ball'. The smoke from the rock is gone, replaced with a 'soft neon blue glow' around the 'original old leather cricket ball'. . .

This strange incident became a great mystery that ironically was the beginning of 'Raji's Storied Sports Career'. . . but it's just the beginning of his life's long path ahead. . .
A 'Path', at that moment, that could 'never' have been imagined.

Chapter 3

Major Kahmal's Protégé

THE VILLAGE - SWAT VALLEY:

Raji is playing cricket with a group of boys. Wickets have been set up to mark the makeshift field of play.

As the boys play, Major Kahmal is at his position on the sidelines coaching and encouraging them.

A slight smile crosses his face as Raji throws pitch after pitch after pitch, with great force and deadly accuracy.

Following the game, Raji and Major Kahmal are walking slowly back toward the village as Kahmal opens up. . .

"Raji, you are quite a hero to our village."

Raji averts his eyes downward. . .

"A true hero is able to save his best friend."

The Major stops, then gently grabs Raji's shoulder and looks directly into his eyes.

"Some things are out of our control, Raji. . .
You no doubt saved the lives of others in the
village. And you did your best, for Adarsh."

"It seems my best was not good enough, Master
Kahmal."

"Adarsh would be proud of how well you play
since that. . . that day.
The ruins seemed to have energized you with a
goodness to 'fight the evil' that threatened us
all."

Raji shrugs. They resume walking.

"Of late, I've noticed something remarkable in
your play, Raji. . . other than, of course, your
amazing natural athleticism. . .
How do you... you seem to be able to focus on the
'most minute spot', then strike that 'target' so
precisely time after time!
It is something that I have never seen, in all my
years."

"But my target is not minute at all, Master
Kahmal."

"I don't understand, Raji . . . the center of the
strike zone, that you hit each and every time, is
miniscule!?"

"But to me it is so 'vast a space', that it would be
impossible to miss, Master Kahmal."

"Let's take a break, Raji. . . I need further explanation and persuasion."

Kahmal heads to a large tree that provides shade from the relentless sun. He sits against the tree trunk. Raji sits next to him as he questions further. . .

"Tell me now, about this 'large target' that is impossible to miss."

"You see, Master Kahmal, no matter how distant an object or its size. . . from the 'eye of a bird' to a 'far-away mountaintop'. . . my vision is filled with that 'spot' and that 'spot', only. I am unable to see anything else. . ."

"So what you are saying is that this 'spot', this 'very small target', which is your focus and aiming point is 'all' that is visible to you?"

"It is like a 'giant eye' that is all around me and determines the 'pinpoint of my aim'. . .
In fact, my mother has said to me, that it is the 'God Shiva's Third Eye'."

"This ability can only be described as the 'Gift of a God'. It seems as though the Hindu God Shiva has blessed you, Raji."

"The blessing may have come from Shiva, Master Kahmal, but it was another GOD who bestowed it upon me."

"Another God!?"

"That day in the Ruins... it was the 'God Hanuman' who helped me defeat the terrorists."

Major Kahmal is stunned by his answer. . .

"But how?"

"I felt he was reaching out to me. He needed my help."

"A God needed your help, Raji? You are a Mortal!
Why would a God need your help?
Now it seems to me. . . that your memories may be muddled and that your mind is confusing 'reality with fantasy'."

Raji gets serious and emphatically voices his response. . .

"No, Master Kahmal, 'Hanuman' really needed me. The terrorists were ready to destroy his physical 'Avatar' sitting unprotected in the Hindu Ruins."

Raji looks skyward, thinking . . .

"I felt a connection to him, a force that penetrated deep into my mind and soul. . .
He gave me strength and made me fearless."

Raji thinks, back in time . . .

"Since that day, I find it 'impossible' to miss any mark, Master Kahmal."

Kahmal's eyes are wide with awe and amazement. He takes a breath, a moment to recover, then looks intensely at Raji.

"Hmm. . . 'Hanuman'? Even though I am a Muslim, I know that he is the 'Hindu God of Sport'."

Kahmal pauses, as he considers Raji point. . .

"You are truly a special boy, Raji. . . a special and very blessed boy."

Kahmal smiles and stands. He reaches out his left hand and pulls Raji to his feet.

"It is time for us to head to the 'family dinners' that await us."

Raji looks up at Major Kahmal.

"Has my explanation persuaded you, Master Kahmal?"

Kahmal smiles gently. . .

"I feel more informed and persuaded, than I could have ever imagined."

Raji and Kahmal continue on down the pathway to the village, Kahmal resting his hand on Raji's shoulder.

THE NEXT DAY: The Village Cricket Field.

Raji is among a group of boys gathered around Kahmal. Raji is the smallest of the group.

"You boys have been working hard and are well prepared for our first game."

One of the older Players, Rabar speaks up. . .

"Who starts as pitcher, Master Kahmal?"

Kahmal glances quickly at Raji.

"I... uh... believe that Raji has earned that spot."

Rabar reacts incredulously. . .

"A 'Hindu' boy will be chosen to lead our team?!"

Another senior player, Qaim adds his objection.

"An infidel should not be given such an honor, Master."

Raji hangs his head, averting his eyes from the others players as Major Kahmal rebukes. . .

"I understand your concerns. We are 'all Muslims' here, except for Raji. But we must be honest and recognize his talents. . .
We cannot allow our prejudices to foster defeat."

Another player, Tariq, invokes his father's opinion. . .

"My father says Raji, should be thrown off the team altogether, Master!"

"Your father is a livestock farmer. I don't tell him that he must separate his 'goats from his sheep'. . .
I am your Coach and I say Raji stays. . . and that he will start the game. And that is final!"

Qaim again, starts moaning. . .

"But Master Kahmal, Raji. . ."

Angrily, the Major puts an end to it!

"No more!"

The Muslim boys are silenced, but they are 'not happy'. They 'glare' at Raji, hatred and resentment in their eyes. . .

LATER AFTER TRAINING:

The boys are dispersing and heading back to the village.
Major Kahmal stops Raji. . .

"Raji, you are a wise young man."

"I am grateful that you believe so, Master. . ."

"Am I, placing you in a position too stressful and uncomfortable?"

"As the starting Bowler, Master?"

Major Kahmal 'nods yes'. . .

"I faced the 'Taliban' killers with no fear and only an 'old worn cricket ball' as a weapon. . .

I believe I can deal with the hatred of my young teammates. . . their glares and angry eyes. . . especially, if I lead them to victory."

Kahmal smiles.

Raji turns away and starts to dart off, then stops and turns back to Kahmal. . .

"Master Kahmal, does your support of me likewise, place you in an uncomfortable position?"

Kahmal and Raji exchange an intense look.

"As I said. . . you are a wise young man, Raji."

Raji bows quickly to Kahmal and darts off, as Kahmal watches him, wistful. . . concern on his face.

A DAY LATER: The Village Cricket Field.

Raji and the other boys are practicing, when Saif, the Thirty-Four-Year old, father of Tariq, one of the players that objected to Raji's position, walks up to Kahmal. . .Kahmal greets him. . .

"Greetings, Saif."

"I have come to you, Kahmal, as your Muslim brother, in spirit. My son Tariq has his heart set on being the 'Starting Bowler' in the game tomorrow."

"Tariq knows well, that I have selected another boy for this position, Saif."

Saif's eyes, narrow in anger. . .

"A Hindu boy, Kahmal?"

"A talented 'Pitcher', Saif."

"There is more to coaching than talent, Kahmal.

It is Allah who watches over us and should be honored. . . I believe it has been said that winning isn't everything."

"I couldn't agree more, Saif. But I believe that
Trying to win, is 'Everything'. . .
So, I have assigned the 'Best Bowler' on the team to start. My eyes are 'blind' to his religious beliefs. . ."

Saif glares, at Kahmal. . .

"But 'Allah' is not blind to the favoritism you show an infidel."

Saif walks off in a huff.

Kahmal sighs, then shakes his head in dismay.

Chapter 4

Raji's Emergence

TIME JUMP: Several years later. . .

A Pakistani Cricket Field: The stands are filled with fans. A large banner strung behind the stands reads, 'Regional Finals'. . .

Raji, now 15, and his teammates are playing defense, with Raji as the 'Bowler'. Kahmal is on the sidelines ever-watchful.

Raji bowls out the final batters in quick succession, to end the game in victory.

Raji's teammates celebrate the victory together, as Raji walks off the field alone.

Kahmal catches up with him.

"Congratulations! Once again, your skills astound me, Raji."

"I have your wisdom and guidance to thank, Master Kahmal."

"I am not sure I have had, much to do with it!

It is you who has just won our team 'a spot' at the Nationals in Islamabad."

"You teach us that victory is only possible through teamwork."

Kahmal smiles slightly. He bends down close to Raji, speaking softly. . .

"That is true. But victory is only probable with YOU, in the lead."

TIME JUMP: Several months later. . .

National Cricket Grounds, Islamabad:
Raji and his team are having a pre-final practice game.
Raji pitches the 'Ball', time after time, with unbelievable speed, strength and accuracy as Kahmal watches.
After practice, the boys are gathered around Major Kahmal.

"I am proud of each and every one of you.
The chances are great that victory will be ours in this final match round for the 'Crown of Pakistan'. . .
But our next challenge will be much more difficult. . . the 'World Cricket Matches' against one of the strongest Cricket Teams Worldwide, 'The Indian National Team' in Mumbai, India."

Kahmal smiles at the boys, who are all cheerful,
except Raji, who stands apart from the other
boys and has a dour look on his face.
Kahmal studies him, concerned.

Later, as the team practice ends and the boys go
their separate ways, Kahmal spots Raji and
walks over to him. . .

"I didn't think it possible that you could improve
even more, but today you proved me wrong. . .

You bowled your fast ball around every batter,
hitting those wickets right on!
You're the fastest 'Yorker' I've ever seen!"

"My humble thanks, Master Kahmal."

Raji's face is somber.

"Is there something, that bothers you, Raji?"

Raji lowers his eyes.

"I do not look forward to playing against my
'Hindu' brothers, for the first time at the 'World
Matches', Sir. . .
Whilst I must strive, to lead a team of 'Muslim
Players' who hate the 'Indians' and hate 'Me', as
well. . .
A 'Victory' over my fellow 'Hindus' would be
bittersweet."

Raji bows quickly, to Kahmal, then runs off.

Kahmal is dismayed, as he watches Raji disappear into the crowd.

Later that Night. . .
Raji wakes, with a start. . .
Something is bothering him. He goes to a hidden drawer in his closet, pulls out a 'Talisman'. . . the remains of the 'Original Yellowed Cricket Ball from the Terrorist Attack in the Ruins. . .
He just stares at it. It still has, a faint 'Neon Blue Glow'.

Quietly, Raji issues a warning, 'severely' to himself. . .

"I must bring this to India."

Subsequently, the next day, at the 'National Cricket Grounds', crowds from the various regions of Pakistan 'go wild', as an unknown team from the 'Swat Valley', finally wins the coveted 'Crown' of Pakistani Cricket, 'The Trophy Cup'.

A MONTAGE OF NEWS HEADLINES – Explodes across the Worldwide Internet, as well as on various News Media and TV Channels out of ISLAMABAD, PAKISTAN. . .

'Stage Set for World Cup Finals in Mumbai. . . India vs. Pakistan'

'National Crown of Pakistan Won'

'An Unknown Bowler, Raji Swat burst onto the International Cricket Scene with a Match winning 70 of 37 balls'

The stage is set for Raji, to finally come out of his self-made obscurity. . .

Chapter 5

Raji's First Setback – 'The Horror'

TIME JUMP: Several weeks later...

Pakistani 'Cricket Training Camp'...
Mumbai, India...
It's late afternoon, as a newly added 'Muslim Team Trainer' is leading Raji and his teammates in calisthenics. The boys are doing a grueling set of sit ups as the Trainer announces...

"Last one, boys!"

The boys groan, as they complete the set. Raji stretches out, on the grass. But surprise...
The Trainer shouts out to them...

"Now for the hard work!"

More groans from the boys...

"Three laps around the track and then weight training."

Raji stands and heads to the running track, when suddenly, Major Kahmal approaches him. Kahmal's face is somber...

"Raji, come with me."

Kahmal grabs Raji's arm and walks him away from the track to an alcove near the athletic training rooms. . .

"But, Master Kahmal, I must run to strengthen my endurance."

At once, Kahmal stops at the locker room entrance and pulls Raji to him. . .

"Raji, I regret to tell you this. . . that your sister, Khaldoon, has been attacked, near your home in Pakistan.
Raji . . . shocked, shows serious concern. . .

"Is she. . ."

Major Kahmal reacts, to add more details. . .

"She'll be okay. . .but. . ."

Kahmal pauses, almost in reverence, softly. . .

"She was. . . uh. . . assaulted by a Gang."

"A Gang of. . . 'Muslims', Master?!"

Kahmal lowers his eyes. . .

"Did they violate, 'My Sister'?"

Kahmal's facial expression tells it all . . .

"I fear so, Raji. . .
You must go to her, now! A wayfarer will escort
you. Be with your family. . ."

Raji rushes to his locker, then quickly returns
with a 'Ball-like Object'. It has a faint 'Blue Glow'.
Raji is passionately insistent . . .

"Master Kahmal, you must hold and protect this
for me, until I return."

Kahmal looks intently at 'The Object', as Raji
hands it to him. . .

"This is the 'TALISMAN' you told me of, from the
'Taliban Attack at the Temple Ruins!?"

Kahmal pauses with extreme concern. . .

"I will protect it with my life, until you return,
Raji. . .
Now go comfort your family, young man."

TIME JUMP: A Full Day of Travel later. . .

The kitchen at Raji's Family compound, hidden
deep in the Swat Valley of Pakistan. . .

Raji is seated at the table having lunch with his
mother. He takes a bite of food, then lays his fork
down, as Veena, his Mother, urges him to eat. . .

"You need to eat for your strength, my Son. You need it for the coming Game."

"How can I think of playing the 'Game of Cricket' with these 'Muslim Players' when my big Sister has been subjected to such abuse, from these same people?"

Tears are welling up in Veena's eyes. She steps across the room and looks behind a curtain into another room, watching her violated daughter's labored breathing.
Softly she speaks. . .

"Khaldoon is finally able to sleep, without moans and cries."

Raji's eyes, show his anger. . .

"I hate the Muslims who hurt her, and I hate the Muslims I play with. I shall quit the team and seek revenge on those, who brought harm to my Sister. . ."

"You cannot quit, my Son! Your father was not a quitter. And you alone, must honor his memory."

"My father would also seek 'Justice', for the horrible crime committed against his Daughter."

Veena, gently grabs Raji's hand.

"It could have been worse, Raji."

Raji scowls at her. . . he's intense, angry. . .

"How, Mama?
How could this 'Horror', this vile 'Assault' of my 'Only Remaining Sister' have been worse, than it was?
It will devastate her entire life. . . Her entire future!"

"Raji. . . listen to me. . . one of the Gang Members had a knife at Khaldoon's throat. . . ready to end her life."

Raji's eyes grow wide, with further disbelief. . .

"What?!"

"Another 'Muslim Boy' who was 'NOT' in the Gang, attacked the 'Vile Criminal' and saved Khaldoon's life."

"Who is this 'Boy', this 'Hero'?"

"His name is 'Hamza'. He was stabbed in the struggle to protect her, and he nearly died."

"Hamza?! I know that 'Boy'!"

Raji stands and immediately heads toward the doorway. . .

"Where are you off to, Raji?"

"To see 'Hamza'. . . to thank him and to honor
him. . . and do as 'My Father' would. . .
'Respect Him'. . ."

"He is too ill for visitors, Raji. . .
Besides Master Kahmal has sent word, this Day,
that you 'MUST' return to Mumbai."

"I will return Only for you, Mama. . . Only
because you ask. . . and Only for 'Khaldoon and
My Father's Memory', to fulfill my obligations. . .

You are better at prayer than I, Mama. . .
So please pray for 'Khaldoon' and of course for
'Hamza's Recovery' on my behalf. . ."

"Raji, the 'Gods' love to hear the Prayers of new
voices. . . you must add your own voice, to those
prayers as well. . ."

Raji averts his eyes. . . as he quickly walks out, to
prepare his return, to the 'Team' in Mumbai. . .

Chapter 6

The Talisman

TIME JUMP: A Full Day of Return Travel . . .

The World Matches in Mumbai, India: Spectators are leaving their seats; others are returning with snacks.

Raji is on the sidelines pitching to another player, Wafi, aged fifteen, as the young boy comments. . .

"Why do we have to practice during the break? We've been practicing for weeks!"

Kahmal is nearby, and overhears Wafi.

"This is a long break, Wafi. We can't risk Raji's arm, freezing up."

Wafi rolls his eyes, in frustration. . .

"We all must sacrifice, for 'Prince Raji'!"

Kahmal smiles. . .

"Keep practicing! I'm going to run to the concession stand for a 'cold yogurt'."

Wafi, then whines out his spoilt remark. . .

"How come, we can't go?"

"Because, your 'Snack' follows, today's 'Victory'."

Kahmal, grinning at the obviously over-indulged child, walks off. . .as Wafi ads a final jab. . .

"Guess we better 'Win', or we don't eat."

THE STADIUM CONCESSION STAND:
Kahmal is in line at the main refreshment stand.

Suddenly, several armed men, with black masks covering their faces, appear.
They begin shooting randomly at the fans getting food and drinks, with their automatic AK-74's.

Many are instantly killed or dying.

Kahmal, upon seeing the Gunmen, then turns to protect a young boy, realizing his own choices, but he is caught in a barrage of gunfire and collapses over the child.

One of the 'Lead Terrorists' approaches the dying Kahmal.

Kahmal sees his 'Glowing Fire Red Eyes', and instinctively removes the 'Cricket Ball Talisman', pushing it into the hand of the child he's protecting.
Speaking softly, in his last dying breath, Kahmal orders the small child he's protecting. . .

"Give this to Raji. . . 'The Cricketer'. . .And Run, my child, Run now!"

As the child escapes, Kahmal, almost dead, looks up to see his aggressor. . . his eyes begin to 'FIX' into a 'Death Stare', but not before KESH, the 'Evil Terrorist' faces him. . .yelling. . .

"Where is 'Hanuman's Talisman', old man? You are on MY 'Hallowed Ground', now, Muslim!"

KESH's voice gets even louder. . .

"Hanuman was banished to the 'Valley of Muslim Hell' for ALL TIME. . .
Yet you 'Returned his Spirit', here.
Did you think for one moment, that I would not sense, that the 'Talisman of Hanuman' was now HERE in India."

KESH seems to be able to suspend Kahmal, from immediate DEATH, as he continues. . .

"For bringing him back, you will 'DIE in Horror' for this!

KESH, frantically frisks Major Kahmal for the hidden 'Talisman', then frustrated, fires several more shots into his now, lifeless body, as he turns and disappears into the chaos of screaming 'Game Fans'.

Mumbai POLICE and stadium SECURITY finally arrive at the scene. . .
After a brief shoot out, the police and stadium security forces, that far outnumber the gunmen, shoot and kill most of the remaining Terrorists.

The attack leaves behind blood, misery, carnage and inconsolable sadness in its wake, at the 'Mumbai World Games'.

CONCURRENTLY:

Inside the Stadium at the 'Main Cricket Playing Field', Raji and Wafi are still practicing. . .

But stop, when they notice that hundreds of fans and spectators are rushing out of the stands, plus, other players who were also practicing, are running off the Playing Field.

Raji reacts first. . .

"What is going on?"

Wafi comments back, sarcastically. . .

"I don't think they're making a run on 'Samosas and Chilies', Raji."

LATER: In the Team Locker Room. . .
Raji and the other players are huddled together as a 'World Match Official', addresses them.

"There was an attack, a 'Terrorist Attack', occurring at our 'Main Concession Stand'."

Raji looks panicked. He cranes his neck looking for Major Kahmal.

"Due to this attack, the decision has been made to suspend the 'World Match' for a two-month cooling-off period."

There are grumbles, throughout the room, from the Boys and their Trainers.

"I have another announcement, however. . .

. . . it is with great sadness, that I must tell you boys that your Coach, Major Kahmal, was among those killed in the attack, that took place at the concession stand.

Tears well-up in Raji's eyes. Wafi's face is stoic. Wafi, then whispers to Raji. . .

"He should have waited with us, for his snack."

Raji drills a hole in Wafi's face, as he thinks. . .
'I hate this Muslim idiot!'

The Official adds a final comment. . .

"Be proud of Major Kahmal, boys. He sacrificed his own life to save a little boy from certain death. He died a hero."

Raji again stares viciously at Wafi. His intense anger growing. . .
Then, Raji pleads to the official. . .

"Sir, who were the killers?"

The Official points to a Police Commander that just entered the room, for comment. . .

"We don't have their names yet, but they apparently were 'Modi Hindu Activists' that have attacked 'Muslims' inside of India, before."

Raji's eyes grow wide. He's stunned into silence.

Wafi whispers, another biting word, to Raji. . .

"Thought they were Muslims, didn't you."

Raji averts his eyes, that are filled with even more sadness and disbelief.

Suddenly, a young 'Hindu Indian Boy' appears at the locker room door.
He asks for 'The Cricketer'.
Someone points to Raji, as he runs over to him.

Instantly, he hands Raji 'The Talisman'. . .

Then speaks softly, almost in a panic, as he looks in fear, around the room at all the 'Muslims'. . .

"The 'Old Man' with one arm saved me. He said to give you this, Sir. . .you ARE 'The Cricketer' are you not!?"

Nodding 'Yes', Raji's face flushes with embarrassment, then foreboding, as the small 'Indian Boy' disappears out the doorway. . . before he can say anything to the child.

Raji then looks at 'The Talisman', as the 'Blue Neon Glow' returns to it. . . then, quickly he hides it in his equipment bag. . .

Chapter 7

The Sports Agent

TIME JUMP: Several Weeks after returning to Pakistan . . .

**We are looking at Hamza's Family Hut in the high altitude zone of the Swat Valley.
It's afternoon, as Raji makes his way up, to finally see Hamza. . .**

**As Raji arrives, an older boy of sixteen is lying in bed, a large bandage around one forearm.
A curtain is all that protects his room, as Raji pokes his head in. Hamza smiles.**

"Come in, Raji, and sit at my sickbed."

Raji walks over and plops into a chair next to Hamza's bed. . .

"Praise the 'Gods' for your recovery, Hamza. I owe you the gratitude of My Father and my family. You saved 'My Only Sister'."

"You would do the same for my Sister, Raji."

"In all honesty, I have not always felt, that way. . . .You have always been fair, Hamza, but the other Muslim boys. . ."

"I know, Raji. Life is difficult in the 'Swat' for a Hindu. . ."

"But now... a fine 'Muslim Boy', has saved my Sister's life. . . That's incredible!"

Raji grabs Hamza's good hand and kisses it.

"I realize now that there are 'Good Muslims and Bad Muslims' . . . I'd say more 'bad than good'."

Raji's looks up with a twinkle in his eye.

Hamza laughs. . .

"I tease you, Hamza."

"Raji, there are 'Good and Bad' Muslims and 'good and bad' everything. . ."

Raji looks off in the distance, thinking. . .

"You know, Hamza, I learned in the worst way possible, that there are also 'Good and Bad Hindus', too. . ."

"True, but I'd say, 'More Good than Bad', Raji."

Raji and Hamza share a laugh, then a warm smile at each other. . .as Raji adds. . .

"Master Kahmal. . . he was 'The Good Muslim'.

I feel shame, that he was killed by Hindus, very 'Bad', maybe even 'Evil' Hindus."

"He was 'My Coach', too, Raji."

Hamza pauses, thinking back of his Master. . .

"Of course, he wasn't able to bring me to your level of 'Play'. . .
I hear that you are being called, 'The Cricketer'."

"I don't deserve that honor, Hamza. That title really belongs to Master Kahmal."

Raji thinks of the 'last words' he had with Master Kahmal, about the 'Team Spirit' needed for a Mumbai 'Victory'. . .

"I once lacked the 'Spirit to Lead' my team of Muslim players, to Victory against my Hindu brothers, but now things have changed."

The two are silent for a moment. Raji stands.

"I must go now, Hamza. . .back to Mumbai."

Hamza smiles at him, knowing. . .

"Win the 'Final Game' for us, Raji!"

"I shall, Hamza. I'll win the 'World Cup' for You, for My Sister, and mostly for 'Major Kahmal'."

TIME JUMP: Later that Night at his Home . . . Raji goes to the hidden drawer in his closet and places 'The Talisman of the Cricket Ball' back in its hiding place. Again, a faint 'Neon Blue Glow' comes back to its color.

Raji muses softly to himself. . .

'Something 'Evil' always happens, when 'The Talisman' is NOT 'Glowing Blue' . . . The 'God Hanuman' must be protecting it, but only when it remains in hiding.'

. . . then prepares to go, into a deep sleep. . .

'The Cricketer'

TIME JUMP: Two Months later in Mumbai, India at the re-scheduled 'World Cricket Match'. . .

A SERIES OF SHOTS – 'The Cricketer'
The spectators are on their feet as Raji pitches to the last player of the Game, who fans the ball, as it hits the wickets and bowls him out.

The Muslim players celebrate together, as Raji walks off alone.

The new 'Muslim Team Coach', Mr. Fazal, a seasoned Cricket Trainer, Thirty-Five Years of age, catches up with Raji walking back to the lockers alone. . .

"An 'Absolutely Phenomenal Match', Raji. . .

You made 'World Match History', today. . .
Raji, you bowled out more players in that last
Game, than ANYONE in the 'World Cricket'
Record Books. . .all the way back to the 1920's."

Raji reacts, but somewhat saddened. . .

"It was really a 'VICTORY' for Master Kahmal."

"So are you ready for the next match, Raji?"

"Of course, Master Fazal. We'll win them all."

As Raji and Fazal begin walking off the field to
the locker room, a Team Trainer catches up with
them. . .

"Mr. Fazal, there's a 'Sports Writer' from the
'World Cricket Magazine' in the locker room
waiting to see Raji. . .
Do you want to meet with him?"

Fazal looks at Raji. . .

"What do you think, Raji. . .
Should we meet with him?"

Raji shrugs, almost nonchalant. . .

"This could be your 'Big Break', Raji. . .
 . . . Let's. . . do it!"

TIME JUMP: A Week Later in Raji's 'Swat Valley' compound. . . his Bedroom . . .
Raji is asleep. He is tossing and turning.

A DREAM SEQUENCE:

Kahmal comes to Raji in his dream. . .
Raji is standing on a misty green Playing Field,
when the ghostly image of 'Kahmal' appears.

'I am proud of you, Raji.'

'I sometimes feel lost. I miss your guidance,
Master Kahmal.'

'There is no missing me, Raji. My spirit will
always be with you. . . Do not become
disillusioned. You must dig deep to find the
resolve to keep going.'

Suddenly, the image of 'Kahmal' fades, as Raji
tries to bring him back. . .

'Master Kahmal. . . Master Kahmal!'

Raji looks all around for 'Kahmal', who is gone.

BACK INTO REALITY: Raji wakes with a start.
He hangs his head for a moment, then sits up
erect, recalling something. . .

He goes to the hidden drawer in his closet, pulls out the remains of the 'Cricket Ball' from the terrorist attack, holds it and stares at it, remembering. . .
It still has a faint 'Neon Blue Glow'. . .

TIME JUMP: A Week Later at a Cricket Training Field in Central Pakistan. . .

Coach Fazal watches on the sidelines, as Raji again leads their team to a 'Victory' over a Regional Rival. . .

The boys run off the field, jubilant, as Coach Fazal focuses on Raji. . .

"Your Third 'No-Hitter' in a row. . . How do you do it, Raji?"

Raji just shrugs his shoulders. . . then casually, he seems to be speaking to the Sky. . . as. . .

"I have more help, than you know, Coach."

Fazal is clearly befuddled with this Kid. . .

TIME JUMP: Two years later, 'The Swat Valley'.

The 'Swat Family' compound's kitchen, it's Raji's
Birthday. . .
Raji, Veena and Khaldoon are eating dinner.

Khaldoon opens with her ardent remark. . .

"You are 'really famous' these days, Brother.
Everyone at the shop knows of you.
They call me the sister of 'The Cricketer'."

Veena adds. . .

"I am so proud of you, Son."

"I appreciate the fame and your pride Mother
but. . . I make so little money. . . I dream of
earning enough, to move us to a 'safer place', like
England or the United States."

Khaldoon jokes to him. . .

"That is a 'dream', Raji. That will never happen."

At that exact moment, there's a knock on their
Hut's front door. Raji runs over and opens it.
Standing in the blowing 'Himalayan Wind' is
Master Fazal, who appears breathless.

"I ran, all the way up here, Raji. . .
I was just contacted by a . . . by a . . . ah"

"By a what, Fazal?!"

"By a Top International 'SPORTS Agent', Raji. He wants to. . . to. . ."

"To WHAT. . . spit it out, Master?!"

"To fly you to England. . . "

"Fly me to England? Why and Who is this Guy?"

"He's NOT British, he's an 'American Sports Agent'. . .
He wants to fly you to England for something 'BIG'.
He read that Article in 'The Indian Cricket Magazine' about YOU last year.
He actually wants you. . .
to try-out for 'Baseball', Raji. . . for. . .
'American Major League Baseball'!"

Veena, and even the 'usually cynical' Khaldoon 'SCREAM' together in delight. Both run to Raji and embrace him.
Raji himself is shocked and astounded. . .
unable to speak a word. . .

'Wembley Stadium'

Chapter 8

The Wembley 'Big Break'

TIME JUMP: Travel to London, England . . .
We enter the colossal Wembley Stadium outside
London, near Twickenham. . .

On this evening, the largest 'Sports Venue in
Britain' is deserted and illuminated only by soft
spotlighting, that marks the massive physical
structure, against the dark night. Its retractable
dome is in place; its iconic lattice arch looms
above.

The field is in total darkness.

When suddenly, the updated and ultra-bright 'Stadium Lights' are turned on sequentially around the entire Stadium interior. . .

Standing alone, in the middle of the green Field, is Raji, appearing smaller and frailer than ever before, in contrast to the gigantic edifice that surrounds him.
The Trainers have placed an 'American Baseball Glove', on his catching hand, as . . . Raji, stunned. . .
looks all around taking in the splendor of the moment.

Hurrying onto the field toward Raji is 'Ron Givens', a Fortyish, well-known 'FINDER' type of 'American Sports Agent'. . .
Coach Fazal, who accompanied Raji to England, is running close behind Ron.

Ron smiles as he approaches Raji. . .

"Now that we're not in the dark anymore, we can see what you've got, Raji . . .
I've heard phenomenal things about you, verging on the supernatural. . .

Raji remains silent, but upon hearing 'supernatural', he lowers his eyes. . .humbled as Master Fazal jumps in . . .

"This small boy will 'surprise you', Mr. Givens."

"Hey. . . Please, just call me Ron. . .When I read that 'Cricket' article about the 'Pakistani Phenom', I had to see him for myself. . .

Raji. . . Coach Fazal. . . I can't thank you 'Both' enough for coming. Maybe I'm wrong, but I feel there's. . . 'magic in the air' tonight."

"Ron, there has definitely been 'magic' in our 'Pakistani Air'. . .
So, perhaps Raji brought some of that 'magic' with him here."

Again, more sheepish, Raji lowers his eyes.

Coming from the dug-out area, 'out of the blue', Raji spies a very large 'American Baseball Player'.

It's Jack Smithson, late Twenties, a professional baseball player, in full uniform and fully equipped, emerging onto the field. Jack is tall and very muscular.
Ron reacts and waves him over. . .

 "Raji, this is 'Jack Smithson'. He'll be catching for you. He's a professional 'Catcher' with the 'Houston Astros', and they're a Team in what is called the 'American League West Division'.

Jack hurries over to them. He flips up his catcher's mask, looking surprised to see 'Little' Raji. . .

"This the 'Boy'. . . er. . . 'Young Man' we're trying out?"

"This is Raji, Jack."

Raji 'nods' to Jack, who continues to look puzzled.

Ron glances over to Fazal.

"And this is Mr. Fazal, Raji's 'Cricket Coach'."

Jack nods at Fazal, who smiles, excited!
Then, Jack questions tentatively. . .

"Did you say, Coach!?"

Jack who towers over Raji and Fazal, looks at the diminutive Fazal and again at the very small Raji, as he appears to be even more befuddled. . .

"So, this is. . . a different 'Try-Out' of sorts. . ."

Ron grins back at him, then shakes his head 'yes'.

"Okay, then, Folks. . . let's get this event going. . .

And Raji, I just want to make sure. . . Do you feel comfortable. . . Do you need anything?"

"I am fine, Sir. . . though. . ."

Raji holds up his 'Catching' hand, burdened by the American styled fielding glove. . .

". . . I'm not accustomed to wearing a 'large leather GLOVE', like this on my hand."

"It's regulation, Raji. Besides, you'll need that for Jack's throwbacks. He's got quite an arm."

As Jack pipes in, to tout his accolades. . .

"Had the 'Second Best Record' for throwing out base runners last season, Raji. . .
. . .I'll go easy on the kid, Ron. . ."

As Ron rips back, at him. . .

"From what I've heard, I Just hope he goes easy, on YOU, Jack."

Jack grimaces. . . "Huh?"

Ron slyly smiles at Fazal, knowingly. . .

While, Raji at last, comments casually!

"Sir, I, of course, shall need a ball. . ."

Ron adds a final question to Raji. . .

"You ever 'Pitched a Baseball', before?"

"No . . . I have only 'Bowled' Cricket Balls."

Jack again frowns. . .

"He's an 'Alley Bowler'? . . . Gawd Almighty!"

Ron laughs a little, then smiles at Jack's funny 'American Bowling Alley' remark . . . reminding him to get set up. . .

"Jack, go ahead and get in position. You'll have the honor of throwing 'Raji' the very first. . . 'Hard' . . . 'Baseball', he's ever held in his hands, but I got the feeling it won't be his last."

Almost nonchalantly, Jack shrugs it off. . .

"Whatever you say, Ron. It's your 'Dime'."

As Jack starts to run off, Ron adds a final. . .

"Hey, Jack. . . Put your mask down. I don't want to pay for your 'broken nose', too."

Jack just chuckles, then glances at Raji. . .

"Pretty sure. . . I won't need it."

Jack trots back a distance of sixty-one feet, equivalent to that exact length, between a Professional Pitcher's 'Mound and Home Plate'.

An impromptu 'Home Plate' has been situated on Wembley's Giant Field. . .

Jack heads over and positions himself behind 'it'.
Plus, Ten-Feet further behind 'Home Plate' is a
solid brick 'back-stop'. . .

Not knowing Raji's instincts, Ron decides to add
his own instructions. . .

"Oh, and Raji, when you throw, focus on Jack's
'Glove'. . .
In baseball, the 'Catcher' gets the call from the
manager and positions his 'Glove' to take
delivery of a ball that's either inside or outside or
maybe to nab a fast ball or even a slider. . .

. . .Sorry, I'm getting too deep in the weeds. I'm
sure you know how to focus on a 'Target' area."

"I have 'certainly' had that experience, Master
Givens."

Fazal chirp's in . . .

"If Raji, has a 'Secret Weapon'. . .
 The 'Target' is exactly that, Ron."

Ron looks at Fazal 'a little puzzled' for that
moment, at least. . .
Then he adds one further item. . .

"We didn't set up a 'pitching mound', which
you'd normally have in regulation play. . .
Not having it may put you at a slight
disadvantage."

Now, Raji spits back a quick question. . .

"What's a 'Pitching Mound', Sir?"

It's where the 'Pitcher' is located. The actual 'pitcher's mound'. . . is the raised 'spot' in the baseball diamond, where the pitcher stands. It gives the pitcher the best throwing angle."
. . . It also helps, with ball speed because the pitcher is throwing slightly downward.
Besides, a 'Baseball' is smaller than a 'Cricket Ball', so that should also, give you some added speed. . .

Ron and Fazal start to walk off, as Fazal adds. . .

"Good Luck, Raji. Although you don't need my good wishes!"

"But they are always 'welcomed', Master Fazal."

Raji and Fazal exchange a knowing smile, as the two gentlemen head for the sidelines.

At a good distance from Raji, Ron says in a whisper, to Fazal. . .

"I'll bet, he's nervous."

As Raji's acute hearing kicks in, he looks back from the Field at them. . . and adds loudly. . .

"I'll bet, he's not."

At that, Ron looks curiously at Fazal. . .

On the Field, Raji spins around his arm a few times to warm it up, Ron and Fazal stand on the sidelines next to an electronic device.
Ron gestures to it.

"This 'Radar Gun' will automatically capture his 'Ball' speed. . ."

Fazal stares at all the high tech 'Player Monitoring' equipment used at the advanced Wembley Sports Center.

"All we had in Pakistan, Ron, were our eyes. If we 'couldn't see his ball', we knew it was fast.

Back out on the field, Jack picks up a ball from a nearby wire basket.

Jack shouts forcefully to Raji. . .

"Ready, Guy?"

Raji nods 'Yes'. . .

Jack throws the ball to Raji. It is thrown with great power and 'snaps loudly' when it impacts Raji's glove. Raji shakes off the sting.

Jack smiles to himself, proud of his display of power.

Raji looks at the baseball, then looks to the sidelines, with both Gentlemen there. . .

Then Raji adds one further item. . .

"You know, Mr. Ron, judging from this 'Baseball' Jack threw me, it's lighter and less dense than my 'Cricket Ball', and so therefore, much easier to strike with a 'Bat', than a 'Cricket Ball. . .'"

Ron looks at Fazal. . . He's amazed at Raji's technical perception. . . then the Coach looks at Raji. . .

Watching, once again, how Raji begins applying his own unique way of focusing on an object.

On the field, Raji, continues for several moments looking and analyzing the smaller 'Ball', the throwing 'Distance' and the 'Target' . . . Jack's 'Baseball Glove'.

Then at once, all of Raji's 'Mind and Eye' are focused on 'The Glove'. . .
. . . 'Jack's Catcher's Mitt'. . .
For the young 'Cricketer', nothing is visible other than 'Jack's Mitt', as far as his eye can see.
Like a 'Laser Beam', he's centered on 'the vanishing point' in the middle of Jack's Glove. . .
It's like he's almost in a trance. . .It's super-human. . . Only the 'Target' matters. . .

Jack is used to quick reaction pitching, he's
clearly frustrated with the timing. . .

"Come on, Man . . . Toss me One. . .
Hey, you want me to move up, a few yards?"

Ron, seeing Jack's impatience, reacts to Fazal.

"The lighter 'Baseball' may not carry, as far as
his usually do, with no training in pitching
baseballs or on the approach and wind up."

But the 'Viewing Judges' are all caught by
surprise, as Raji rears back to throw. . . does his
own version of a wind-up, then scalds the ball at
'Rocket Speed' into Jack's Glove. . .

Ron chokes. . .

"Oh, my God! Did you see that?!"

Fazal simply chuckles. . .

"My point exactly. . . it was too fast, to even see!"

Ron's still reacting . . .

"If he was pitching on a mound, Gawd knows
how fast it would have been!"

On Jack's end, he was not prepared for such a
powerful delivery. . . and is taken aback in shock.

Jack seethes closed mouthed to himself. . .

"Jesus!"

Jack's eyes are wide with amazement. He quickly snaps his 'Catcher's Mask' back down. He doesn't want a broken nose after all, 'Thanks Ron'.

On the sidelines, Ron and Fazal look at the reading on the 'Radar Screen'. Ron looks at Fazal, incredulously.

"Eighty miles. . . Fazal. . . Eighty-miles-per-hour. . . For a 'First Ever Baseball Pitch', that's awesome!"

"That is, truly fast, Sir! We did not have a way to gauge his actual speed with a 'Cricket Ball'. We just called his pitches fast, faster and fastest."

Jack stands, calling out to Ron. . .

"How fast was it, Ron?"

"Eighty-miles-an-hour."

Jack shrugs, then squats back down. He throws the ball back to Raji. . . as he huffs to himself. . . *'I could throw faster than that. . . probably.'*

Ron, then yells out to Raji. . .

"Try another, Raji."

Again, Raji does his version of a windup and throws the ball 'even harder'. . . so fast that it makes the first ball seem slow.
This time it's Jack, who shakes the 'sting off his hand' in his protective Glove, even after impact.

Ron watches more intensely, silently reacting . . . *'Unbelievable'!*

Ron hurries and looks at the radar reading. Then, loudly yells out to Raji and Jack. . .

"Ninety-Seven-miles-an-hour!"

Again, Jack mumbles to himself. . .
'I could throw that fast, if I wanted to. . . probably. . . maybe.'

TIME JUMP: Several Hours at Wembley . . .
Ron has 'Photo Captured', a series of 'Pitches' that exceeded One-Hundred-Miles per hour.

Another fast ball. . .101
Another pitch and an even faster ball. . .101.5

Ron and Fazal look at the 'Radar Screen' and celebrate with big smiles and high-fives.

Jack catches a ball that nearly tips him back on his rear end. He then mumbles to himself. . .
'If this keeps up. . . I'm gonna need a Kevlar insert!'

Finally, Raji is getting ready to throw. . . as Ron reminds him. . .

"Okay, Raji, this'll be your last pitch. Make it a good one. . ."

Raji goes through his focus ritual, then winds up and pitches. Ron checks his numbers. . .

"One-Hundred-and-Seven-miles-an-hour!"

Ron is ecstatic. . .

"Fazal, that is One-mile-per-hour-slower, that the all-time 'Fastest Baseball' ever pitched. . . A 'Hall of Famer', way back in 1974, a Pitcher named 'Nolan Ryan', threw one that was clocked at 108.1 miles-per-hour. . .

That record has stood for all the years since. . . Raji is an eyelash away from breaking that. Oh my God, wait 'til he's trained!"

Coach Fazal is smiling from ear to ear. . .

"I told you this small boy would surprise you."

"Surprised, shocked, stunned, astonished. . . all inadequate words for describing this. . . it's an absolute 'Miracle'.

Jack trots over to Ron and Fazal, as Ron remarks. . .

"So, what do you think, Jack?"

Jack shrugs. . .

"Sign him up, I guess!"

Ron and Fazal smile. . . But, Jack appears a bit perplexed, as he saunters off to the locker rooms.

Ron's smile fades a little, as he looks out at Raji gathering up several baseballs around him on the ground. . .

You know, Fazal. . . Raji has the potential to have one of the most remarkable athletic careers in the history of modern-day sports."

"Ron, I'll tell you a secret. . . if Raji is signed by an 'American Baseball Team', believe me I can speak for all Pakistanis, especially those in the 'Swat Valley', when I say that "Remarkable" will NOT be an adequate enough word, for what he will accomplish."

Ron and Fazal both watch as Raji runs toward them, carrying a pile of baseballs in his 'New Glove' which he is bracing with both hands. . .
 A few fall off the pile. . . he stops and picks them up. . .as Ron wistfully jokes to Fazal. . .

"He looks like a young ball boy, running off the field, after chasing a foul ball. . .

Not the 'Phenom' with Skill and Speed that will send 'shock waves' around the world."

"You have to wonder, Ron. . . he's such a pure spirit, what the 'Life of a Celebrity' might do to him?"

Ron looks intensely at Fazal. . .

"Well, for one thing, make him 'Filthy Rich'."

Chapter 9

A New Beginning: Oakland

TIME JUMP: Phoenix, Arizona - USA . . .
After multiple Fight connections from London,
England, the group has finally arrived in
Phoenix, AZ . . .
The initial 'Tryouts' for The Oakland A's are in
progress at their Spring Training Camp, near the
city of Phoenix. . .

As we arrive on the scene, Baseball players are
tossing balls around, pitching and catching and
practicing their swings.
For the first time, Raji and Fazal walk onto the
field, accompanied by their Agent Ron Givens, as
Raji makes an observation. . .

"So, these Men training here are the 'Oakland
Athletics Team, Mr. Ron?"

"It's their 'Spring Training Camp' prior to
starting their season at the Oakland COSCO
Stadium in California. . .some are signed and
others are trying out, like yourself. . ."

Fazal watches the large contingent of Players, as
they work through various routines. . .

"Why did you choose the A's, Ron?"

"This team is badly in need of a 'Pitching Star'. They haven't won a 'World Series' in Forty-Four years, they currently have the worst overall winning record in American baseball, and their new owners COSCO are 'Billionaires', maybe even 'Trillionaires', that will pay 'Top-Dollar' to re-build the Team. . .
And last, but not least, the A's are in the 'American League', which has the designated hitter rule, so Raji has only to focus on pitching!

Raji immediately is curious. . .

"Tell me more about this 'Designated Hitter' rule, Mr. Givens?"

"Well, Raji, it means the 'Pitcher' doesn't have to bat. The ninth hitter in the line-up is the DH or 'Designated Hitter' instead of the Pitcher."

Fazal, naively adds his 'two-cents'. . .

"Raji is a very good 'Striker', I mean 'Batter'."

There's 'not enough time' to get him up to speed on American Baseball Batting Strategy, too. . .
Let's just stick to 'Pitching' for now. . .

An errant ball comes right to Ron, who catches it. He hesitates, looks at Raji for a moment, then throws the ball back to the Player. . .as
Quietly, he speaks to Fazal. . .

"I thought of letting Raji throw it back, but we don't want to 'ruffle any feathers'. . . just yet."

Fazal speaks out in surprise. . .

"I don't understand."

"If Raji makes the cut, Fazal, there's a good chance he'll outplay the entire pitching staff. . . It's best to keep their 'egos intact' for as long as possible."

But, Fazal still is seeking more reasons for Ron's decision. . .

"So this 'Oakland Team', suits Raji, the Best?"

"Fazal, a successful tryout with the 'Oakland A's' would, if they have any sense, give Raji the best chance for being picked up with any AL Team."

Ron, then turns to Raji. . .

"And, Raji, there is a large population of 'Hindu and Indian' ex-patriots living in Oakland. So, I thought YOU and your family would feel more comfortable and secure there, rather than in other American cities. . ."

Raji offers a rare smile to Ron. . .

"I am gratified, by your interest in the personal comfort of My Family and Me."

THE TRYOUTS: Time forward, several hours. . .

At the 'Pitcher's Mound'. . . Raji stares down his first 'A's Batter'. . . in the Catcher Position, it's Sammy Correa, Twentyish, he's a Signed Player.

Raji focuses on Sammy's 'Mitt'. . . Everything is blocked out, but the very center 'Target Zone of the Mitt'.
But suddenly, the 'Batter' steps out of the box, breaking Raji's spell momentarily.
Raji takes a deep breath, as he watches the Man pause his actions in a 'Time Out'.

The 'Batter' looks down at Sammy. . .

"Since when are you recruiting from 'Middle School at these 'Tryouts'?"

Sammy tries to humor him, not knowing what to expect from Raji. . .

"Step back in, Brother. I'm sure you'll hit the first pitch, way outta here!"

The cocky 'Batter' moves back into the batter's box and again faces Raji. . .

Finally, adjusting to the 'Pitcher's Mound' effect, and with his timing on, Raji focuses with his version of the windup, then delivers his 'First' A's Fast-Ball, which 'Mr. Cocky' swings at and misses. . .

Then 'Mr. Cocky' looks down at Sammy. . .

"Is this some kind of trick?"

Sammy grins at the idiot. . .

"Better Get Ready for the 'Fast Ball'. . . that was, from what I've heard, the 'Kid's' 'Slow Ball'."

"That 'Kid' has got, a 'Strange Wind-Up'."

"Seems to work, though, Don't It."

After another strike-out, a 'Big Hulking' A's Batter steps up to the plate.

Ron immediately, runs out to the 'Mound'. . . Then whispers to Raji. . .

"You might want to change your strategy. . . This is the A's 'Top Batter'."

"I must confess, Mr. Givens. . . that I have only one strategy."

I think you might want to 'Pitch' around this fellow? He can 'smash it' outta here."

"He'd have to hit the 'Ball', first."

Ron smiles. . .

"I think it best, I leave strategy to you, Raji."

Ron runs back off the field, to watch the 'Wizard' Play!

Raji winds up and zings the 'Ball' past the batter.

The 'Big Batter' to the UMP. . .

"I didn't even see that."

The UMP chuckles. . .

"Scary thing. . . neither did I."

The UMP takes off his glasses and holds them up to the sunlight, gazing at them. The batter frowns.

The 'Big Guy' Batter watches the UMP prep . . .

"How are you gonna call this Guy's 'Pitches'?"

"Uh. . . Maybe I'll need some newer specs?"

Another 'Strike-Out, and after several more, the A's Trainer moves in another 'Pitcher' to give the rest of the Team, a chance to 'at least make contact' with some Pitched Balls. . .

TIME FORWARD: An Indian Restaurant in downtown Phoenix - Early Evening . . .
Raji, Ron and Fazal are eating dinner, as Ron takes the stage first. . .

"So, Raji, how do you feel about. . . everything?"

"In no way do I intend to be boastful, but I feel I can bring skills to the Oakland Athletics, that will make a trip to the World Series possible."

"I think you're being modest, Raji."

"Modesty is an asset in my world, Mr. Ron. I have but one concern. . ."

Ron waits for more information. . .

"American culture is so vastly different from what I have known. I do not question whether I can make the transition from a 'Cricketer' to a 'Baseball Player'.

That I feel assured of. . . But I have doubts that I and my Family can adjust to the American culture. . . of their style of living life so obsessed with material objects and selfishness . . ."

"Raji, That's why I thought Oakland with its large population of 'East Indians and Hindus' would be a plus for You and Your Family."

Fazal then adds his own perspective. . .

"If you make the team, Raji, you will be welcomed by our people with open arms in Oakland and around the world. . .

You would be treated as an idol by your fellow countrymen."

Raji just shrugs at that thought. . .

"Of course, it's all just talk and fantasy, if the Oakland Athletics fail to offer me a contract."

Raji looks intensely at Fazal and then at Ron neither of whom have a response.

TIME FORWARD: An upscale Hotel outside Phoenix near Scottsdale at Camelback Mountain. . . . Late Night.

In the darkened room Raji is asleep in his bed and Fazal is asleep in the room's other bed, when the phone rings. Fazal gropes for the handset. He's mumbling, to himself. . . *'Who calls at this hour?!'*
Sleepily, he picks the phone up. . .

"Yes?" . . .
(He listens) . . .
"Really?" . . .
 (listens) . . .
"Of course, I shall tell him at once."

Fazal hangs up the phone, pulls the covers back over his head and rolls over. . .

Suddenly, he jerks up abruptly. His eyes widen and a smile begins to cross his face. . .loudly, he shouts. . .

"Raji. . . RAJI!"

Raji stirs and moans. . .

"Raji. . . you are an 'Oakland Athletic'!"

Finally, Raji sits up leaning on one arm. . .

Like coming out of a trance. . . he reacts!

"I'm a what?!"

"The Oakland A's have picked you up!
You are an 'American Major League' Baseball Player. . .
You have made their roster for the '2034 Season'
. . . as a 'Relief Pitcher'!
'Raji Swat' from the 'Swat Valley in Pakistan' is an American Major League Ball Player! Wow!"

Fazal can hardly contain himself. He gets up and begins pacing. . .

"And, Raji, not only will you be a professional athlete, you will be a 'very wealthy young man'!"

Raji gazes off in the distance, his face stoic, taking it all in.

Raji, to himself, quietly recites his longed for wish. . .

'Now, I'll be able to provide a 'Safe Place' for my Mother and my Sister. . . I shall send for them at once. . .'

Chapter 10

Baseball Season 2034

TIME JUMP: Oakland, California - USA . . .

We now arrive in the massive 'COSCO Stadium' owned by 'China Ocean Shipping Company', the World's Largest Container Shipping Enterprise.

Currently, COSCO also owns the entire 'Port of Oakland, California' and has just built the largest and most technically advanced Baseball Stadium in America.

There it will house their newly acquired 'Oakland A's', formally known as the 'Athletics' and previously located in Las Vegas, Nevada.

COSCO has also completed a 'High-Speed' Rail Freight Line, connecting Oakland to Chicago via Denver utilizing a 'Direct Under-The-Rockies' Tunnel System that boasts the 'World's Longest Underground Tunnel' (Sacramento to Denver @ 1,900 kilometers).

It's Opening Day of 'Baseball Season 2034'. . . Once again diminished by the sheer size of the massive COSCO Stadium, Raji walks alone onto the green outfield, as he heads toward the 'Bullpen'.

As he moves along, he hears a rush of cheers off to his right. The cheering is coming from the field box that Veena and Khaldoon are seated in.

He gives them a quick glance, but remains stoic. Veena and Khaldoon are surrounded by other Pakistanis, who are there to support Raji.

Just before stepping into the bullpen where other Relief Pitchers are already situated, Raji turns back and takes in the huge modern COSCO Stadium where he will be playing.

Raji is finally able to smile and enjoy this one moment, as he absorbs his success and where it has taken him.

The cheers and applause of the spectators are at times deafening.

Raji sits alone on the end of one of the benches. The other relief pitchers are all gathered together at the other end of the bench.

One of the Relief Pitcher's spies Raji and tries to antagonize him. . .

"Hey, kid. How old are you, anyhow?"

"I'm Eighteen years old."

The Relief Pitcher, then turns to one of the others and takes a jab. . .

"Eighteen? He looks like he's Twelve, Mike!"

Raji holds his head high, as the other Players have a laugh at his expense. . .

Another Player piles on laughing. . .

"Are you a Muslim, Boy?"

The First Relief Pitcher, jumps back in for a gut punch. . .

"Muslims are terrorists, Right?"

Raji tries to clarify, but it doesn't help. . .

"I am Hindu."

Finally, Mike, the other Relief Pitcher, gets some more flesh. . .

"They're 'Terrorists', too. Right?"

"I'm not a Terrorist. I'm a Baseball Player in 'America'! It's just that I'm from Pakistan, that's my Homeland."

The First Relief Pitcher, then walks closer to Raji and stands directly in his face. . .

"You might be a Baseball Player in America, but you're not an 'American'."

"That's true, Sir. . . I am a loyal 'Pakistani', who greatly admires 'America'."

Relief Pitcher Mike, decides to add-on one more, to the other snide comments. . .

"Sounds like you'd rather be in 'Pakistan', Boy. Why'd you even come over here and leave 'that place' anyway. . ."

"Actually, Sir, I was quite content in 'Pakistan'. It seems this 'Team' needed me, more than I needed it."

Both Relief Pitcher's glare angrily at Raji, shaking their heads at his 'spot on' and obviously 'accurate' remark. . .

TIME JUMP: Game Over - Later That Night, at the 'Team Locker Room' Entrance . . .

Outside, the Stadium is beginning to thin out.

Ron trots over to the Locker Room, as Raji emerges. He is the last to leave. The other 'Relief Pitchers' are already walking away together in a group, talking and laughing.

"Got your 'First Game' under your belt, Raji. Too bad it was a loss."

"But I did nothing, other than warm up, Ron."

"You'll get your chance. . . If they're smart, they'll give you that chance, real soon, Raji."

"It may be smart, but may not be wise."

Ron waits for more feedback. . .

"The other players already hate me, call me a 'Terrorist', a 'Dot Head' and basically, tell me to 'go back from whence I came'."

"Hey, Raji, I'm very sorry about that. . .
But it'll 'blow over'.
They'll forget all about it, once you show them your 'Game Skills'."

"Though, I can't say that I will, Mr. Ron."

Raji speeds up and runs the rest of the way to the 'Players Only' Exit Gate, leaving Ron shaking his head, concerned.

TIME JUMP: Downtown Oakland at a Popular Indian Restaurant, Later that Night . . .
Raji is with Veena and Khaldoon and several other 'Pakistani Hindus' who cheered him on at his 'First Game'.

There is a celebratory mood all around, however, Raji is distracted, lost in thoughts and sober-faced. . .

Veena quietly tries to bring him out of his punk.

"Raji, you need to join in the 'Fun'. Everyone is here for you. You must come out of your shell and celebrate with everyone."

"Mama, there is nothing for me to celebrate. I didn't even play!"

"But we celebrate your new home, Raji. . . your new beginning, your fabulous 'New Career'!"

Khaldoon is listening in, she senses his pain. . .

"I know how he feels, Mama. He feels he has not earned 'The Praise' of his Countrymen, yet."

"Exactly, Khal'D, I have let them all down."

Veena gently grabs Raji's arm. . .

"You have let absolutely NO ONE down! And don't you ever think otherwise. . ."

Khaldoon tries to smooth over his feelings. . .

"You'll prove yourself, Raji. We all know you have the 'Talent', just remember you're. . .
 'The Cricketer' and they have yet to really see what you can do with a 'Baseball'. . ."

Veena jumps in too. . .

"And if your 'American Coaches' have any sense at all, they will put your skills to use soon, if they truly want to have a 'Victorious' Season."

Raji continues to avert his eyes, thinking. . .

Chapter 11

Agent verses Manager

TIME JUMP: Manager's Office – COSCO Stadium. . . A partially closed door bears a brass plate that reads, 'Duke Larson, Manager'. . .

Oakland A's manager, Duke Larson, late Fifties, is seated at his desk reviewing re-plays on his various computer screens, when there is a knock on his door.

He looks up to see Ron Givens standing in the threshold. . .

"Got a minute, Coach."

Duke looks flustered, as he glances at the video playing and the stacks of files and papers on his desk.

"Thirty seconds, tops, Ron. . .but come on in!"

Ron hurries in.

"Just thought, I should bring something to your attention."

"This about your, 'Dot-Head'?"

Ron sighs heavily. . .

"It is, Coach. . . and it's about calling the 'Kid'
Names. . ."

"What? . . . 'Like Dot-Head'. . ."

Ron 'nods' in agreement. . .

"Look, Ron, I don't have anything against the
'Kid', but with all the 'Crap' I gotta do. . ."

Duke gestures to his messy desk. . .

"And this new Ownership from 'China'. . ."
Let's face it. . . it's just another 'Young Feller'
that I have to teach the 'Ropes' to. . . and at the
same time baby the little 'Paki'."

Ron winces at the word, 'Paki'. . .

"Deal with it, Ron. . . if he can't take, the 'good-
natured' ribbing of his 'Team Mates' and the
other 'Relief Pitchers'. . ."

"Hah. . . It's not good natured, Duke. . .
It's cruel, obnoxious and intentionally hurtful.

. . . The other players aren't interested in
bringing him into the fold. Raji knows it and I
can see it on their faces. . .
They don't want anything to do with him, and
there's clearly an element of envy. . ."

Duke angrily reacts. . .

"Envy?! . . . My boys don't resent the 'Kid's'
abilities. . ."

"I'll be glad to debate that assumption at another
time, Duke, but bottom line is . . . they do resent
him and his very 'presence' here. . .

Funny. . . You say Your 'Boys' don't resent him,
try to remember that 'Raji' is. . . one of 'Your
Boys', Now. . ."

"Fact is, Ron, as you well know, I 'have to
improve' my 57 - 105 record from last year. . .

If I don't, I'm GONE, and so are most of the
current and new Players, including 'Raji'. . .

So you see, I have much more to worry about
than that skinny little 'Indian Kid' with a good
arm. . ."

". . . I'd say a 'Great Arm'. . . and currently,
an 'Un-Tested' Arm in 'American League'
Division Play!"

"Fine, then . . . a Great Arm.
But the 'Kid' is just a 'Relief Pitcher' among a
group of 'Seasoned Relief Pitchers', who have
'much more experience' than he does. . ."

Duke moves his keyboard to one side. . .

"Ron. . . I have starting pitchers - some good, some overrated - infield and outfield ballplayers of varied talents - good batters and horrible batters.
. . . Frankly, I don't have the time to 'baby' the 'Kid', because you think he's being treated harshly. . . for Christ's sakes, Ron, this isn't called the 'BIG LEAGUES' for nothing!"

"Well, Duke. . . Not that you want my advice or will take it, but you are really screwing up, if you don't give this 'Kid' the chance he deserves. . .
. . . He could take you to the 'Series'."

Duke laughs, dismissively. . .

"I've heard that 'Joke' before. . . your 'thirty seconds', are up, 'Pal'."

"The 'Kid'. . . 'CAN WIN' for you, Duke."

Ron turns on his heel to leave, quite miffed. When he reaches near the door, he stops and turns back around toward Duke, for one more jab. . .

"Speaking of 'Boys', Coach. . . I think you and 'Your Boys' should all grow up. . .

'Real Men', know how to deal with things that aren't in the 'Player's Handbook'. . ."

Ron hurries to the door and leaves.

Duke, unmoved, watches him leave.
Then wads-up the piece of paper he's holding in
his hand and throws it at the Door 'after Ron', as
an aggressive afterthought. . . hissing to himself.

*'Raji one of My Boys, my ass?! . . . My Boys
aren't Dot Heads.'*

Duke returns to his computer video screens, and
the amassed pile of work, staring him in the face.

Chapter 12

The 'Bullpen' Call

TIME JUMP: COSCO Stadium. . . Oakland, California. . . Five Weeks Later. . .

A Night Game. . . Fourth Inning
Score - Kansas City Royals - 2 : Oakland A's - O.

The Stadium is packed. It's Early in the Season, but it's looking bad for Oakland in the 'Win' column, already. . .

The massive COSCO Stadium lighting system has turned the 'Green Playing Field' and the 'Diamond' into a perfect un-shadowed environment for professional baseball. . . It's considered the 'Best Playing Field' in America!

'A's' BULLPEN: Raji sits at the far end of one of the benches with another relief pitcher, Sergio, a Twenty-Four year-old, Hispanic Player, from the Dominican Republic. . .
The other relief pitchers, a much larger group, are clustered together at the other end of the bench. . .

Sergio decides to talk to Raji, since the other Pitchers seem uninterested in him. . .

"You from India, Man?"

"You're Close. . . 'Pakistan'."

Sergio 'nods' toward the other group of mainly 'White' Relief Pitchers. . . then almost silently comments. . .

"I think you have to be 'White-Anglo', to join that 'CLUB'. . ."

"Well, that most certainly, leaves me out. . . and I say, good for that, too."

"This is my 'Second Season' here. . . And most of them, don't even know my name."

"You're 'Sergio', Correct! . . ."

"Yes. . ."

"I shall 'always' know your 'Name', Sergio . . . . . . and my name is 'Raji'."

Sergio smiles. . . he's really gratified. . .

TIME JUMP: Scoreboard - Fifth Inning. . .
Score - Kansas City Royals - **4** : Oakland A's - **O**.

Raji and Sergio are standing at the 'Bullpen' wall, watching Kansas City beat the socks off their infield, as the bases go loaded. . .and no OUTS. . .

"Doesn't look good for us, Raji."

Raji just shrugs. . . since he can't do anything about it. . .

Suddenly the ringing 'Bullpen' phone breaks the silence of their thoughts. . . One of the other Relief Pitchers runs over and answers it. . .

"Wow. . . All right. I'll tell them."

The seasoned Relief Pitcher, hangs up the phone, then casually walks up to Raji and Sergio. . .
His face tells it all, 'He's pissed'. . .

"Coach says for you 'Guys' to warm up."

Raji and Sergio look at each other. . .they're astonished, that they, were even considered.

After about, Ten Minutes, with Raji and Sergio in the 'Bullpen' pitching back and forth to one another, they realize the Game has been halted with a 'Time Out' for Media and Television Advertising coverages. . .

OAKLAND DUGOUT: Duke is pacing back and forth, focused on the Field. He has a scowl on his face. . . beads of perspiration have broken out on his forehead.
While, Jake Armstrong, his younger Assistant Coach, is standing nearby for instructions. . .as Duke spits it out. . .

"Looks like we'll be chalking up, 'Loss Number Four. . . with three on base and no outs. . ."

Jake also looks onto the Field, thinking. . .

"Yep. . . Once again, No Batting and No Pitching, How do you get a 'Rally Going', with those Odds."

"Media will be coming back at any minute. . . Who you got warming up, Duke?"

"The 'Little Paki' and the 'Spanish Dude'. This is what it's come down to, Jake. . ."

Jake scans his 'Roster Tablet Screen'. . .

"It's a 'Sad State of Affairs'. . .better start looking for my next 'Play Gig in 2035'. . ."

"Well, since this game is 'Going to Hell' anyway, we might as well see if one of the 'Little Idiots', can 'bring it'."

"Which one, Duke?"

"Does it really 'Matter', Jake?!"

Jake drags out a 'Silver Coin' from his pocket, for just these situations. . . positions it over his 'thumb and four finger', ready to flip it. . .

"Call it, Coach."

Okay. . . It's Heads. . . the 'Spanish Dude'. . . Tails. . . 'The Paki' Wins. . ."

Jake flips the 'Coin". They both, stare at it!

TIME JUMP: Minutes Later at the Bullpen. . .

Media 'Time Out' has ended. . .but Duke has requested a 'Pitching Change Time-Out'

Scoreboard – Top of the Fifth Inning. . .
Score - Kansas City Royals - 4 : Oakland A's - O.

Again, the 'Bullpen' phone rings.

'Relief Pitcher' Mike answers this time. . . He has a brief conversation, then. . .

"It's the 'Paki', Guys. . ."

Mike shouts toward the 'outcasts' at the end of the Bench. . .

"Raji. . . You're up."

Raji's eyes grow wide. Sergio smiles. . .
The 'Paki Kid' is momentarily immobilized.

'Relief Pitcher' Mike, again shouts out!

"GO, Raji!"

Sergio adds his own reinforcement. . .

"Go to it, Man. Show 'em, what you Got!"

Finally, Raji takes a deep breath, picks up his
Glove and with a somber face. . .
He exits the 'Bullpen' and steps onto 'The Intense
Green' of the massively lit-up, 'Nighttime Playing
Field'. . .
Then he makes his aggressive, but lonesome
march to the vacant 'Pitcher's Mound'.

Totally caught by surprise, Ron and Fazal are
sitting in a 'Third Base Field Box', observing
everything. . .
They can't contain their joy, as Raji quickly
approaches the Mound. . .

But Raji doesn't look around, at all.
He acts as though he's in a trance, unaware of his
surroundings. . .

Fazal watches him. . . and reports to Ron, for his
appreciation of these odd actions. . .

"In many ways, he is 'Alone', Ron."

Ron nods his head in agreement, understanding Fazal's explanation. . .

PITCHER'S MOUND: In moments, Duke, Jake and Sammy are all on the Pitcher's Mound with Raji. . . They each tower over him, in a protective huddle. . .

Jake speaks first, his typical encouragement. . .

"It's just the top of the Fifth, Raji. . ."

Duke jabs in his comments, with his somewhat negative approach. . .

"And we're only behind Four Runs. . . we've been in 'much worse shape' before. . . Of course, there're 'No Outs and the Bases ARE Loaded'. . . but you'll find a way. . ."

Jake comes back with . . .his 'focus' thought. . .

"Just Keep your eye on 'Sammy's Glove Target'."

"I always DO. . . Mr. Jake!"

"GAWD, Kid. You always make me sound like a slave owner with YOUR obedience."

Duke adds his 'One Main Thought'. . .

"You got a Great Arm, 'Kid'. But when nerves set in and you're actually on the spot. . . things can change. . .

Finally, Sammy gets in the last word. . .

Just, put it in 'My Glove', Raji. . .I'll mark your 'Target' every time!

"I have no other Goal, Sammy. . ."

It's Time! . . . And the 'Home Plate' UMP is getting antsy, even pacing a bit. . .

Then, the UMP, yells loudly. . .

"Play Ball!"

Duke, Jake and Sammy all hurry off the 'Mound'.

Ron and Fazal in the 'Third Base Field Box' are watching all of this intensely, like two mother hens. They lean forward, on the edges of their seats, silently rooting their protégé on. . .

"It's just Raji's, Luck! He's facing Xander Garcia.

Fazal naively reacts. . .

"I hear he's, Good. . ."

"I'd say he's 'Good', alright. He's last year's AL Batting Champ."

"I'll pray to the 'God Hanuman' on Raji's behalf."

"I don't know who that is, Fazal, but I'll pray to him, as well. . ."

"He's a powerful fellow in the 'Hindu World'."

"I'm glad Raji got a 'little training time' prior to his 'wind up' out there. . ."

"I don't think the 'wind up' is that important for Raji."

Ron looks up and around at the Massive Stadium Crowd. . . As some of the 'part-time' Oakland Fans are starting to leave COSCO. . .

"I hope the 'Fans' who are leaving aren't a distraction to Raji."

"They won't be, Ron. . . he sees nothing, but the 'Center of the Wickets'. . .
I mean 'Catcher's Mitt'. . . .it's his focus, it's like no one else, I've ever worked with in Coaching.

Ron looks at Fazal quizzically. . .

"You've hinted at something like that before. I'd like to learn more about his 'technique'."

"Not sure it's a 'technique', Ron.
It's more, that it's part of Raji's being. . .
. . . I feel sorry for the Fans who are leaving."

"We call them 'Part-Timers or Fair Weather Fans'. . ."

"Yes and they're going to miss the show of their lives and the start of a 'Career', that will begin to skyrocket this very night, Ron."

"I hope you're Right!"

"Just like Raji. . . I have no doubts."

PITCHER'S MOUND: Raji bends over at the waist and focuses like a laser on home plate and the strike zone at Sammy's 'Glove'.
Everything in Raji's sight is blocked except the very center of the 'Catcher's Mitt'.

Raji continues to stare. . .
While, the Batter and the UMP are nervously awaiting his first pitch. . .

DUGOUT: Duke is also growing impatient.
Angrily, he jumps on Jake. . .

"What the hell is he doing?!
Why, doesn't he throw the damned Ball . . ."

Jake, standing next to Duke, turns toward Sammy at 'Home Plate' and makes a series of hand signals. . .
"I just told Sammy to ask the UMP for a time out so we can run out there. . ."

"And find out what the 'Hell' is going on!"

PLAYING FIELD: At 'Home Plate'. . . Sammy turns to the UMP.

"Hey, the 'Kid's' new. . . He's freezing up. . . We need a short talk with him. . ."

UMP without comment. . .shouts loudly. . .

"Time Out!"

Raji sighs and rolls his eyes. . . he was ready. . .

The 'Batter' scowls. . .he was ready. . .
The Batter then, steps out of the 'Box' and turns to the UMP.

"I thought we were playing a 'Major League Team', here!"

UMP finally comments. . .

"Two Minutes 'Only', Sammy!"

Sammy stands up, and trots out to the 'Mound,' just as he is joined by Duke and Jake.
They again surround Raji, in a 'Huddle'. . .

Duke spits it out first. . .

"What's wrong, Kid?"

"Nothing was wrong, until the 'Time-Out' was called, that prevented me from pitching the 'Ball'."

Jake clarifies the Guidelines. . .

"You're taking too long, preparing. . ."

"I only take as long, as necessary, Sir."

Duke growls his dissatisfaction. . .

"You gotta be faster. . ."

"In the long run I will be faster, Coach. . .
My 'Ball' will be 'Fast', and the Inning will be over 'Fast'. . ."

Jake himself, has become frustrated. . .

"You think you're going to 'Strike' everybody Out, but. . ."

Duke jumps in, before Jake can finish. . .

". . . This is the 'BIG LEAGUES', Kid. . .NO MORE DELAYS. . ."

"I'm reminded about that, repeatedly, Coach. . ."

"Speed it up, then."

"Coach, trust me, just this Inning. Let me do things the way 'I know how to do them'."

Raji looks serious, he scans all their faces. . .

"You'll see that, I'm right."

Duke looks equally serious, at Raji . . .

"You realize, that I'm the 'Boss'. . ."

"No doubt, Coach!
But a 'Good Boss', uses his people to the best of their ability.
Just. . . Give me the Inning. . .and I'll make you Proud!"

Sammy suddenly agrees with Raji. . .

"He can do it, Coach. . . I 'Feel' him. . ."

Duke looks intensely at Jake, who shrugs.

"Well, we're Losing anyway. . . Four to Zip, No Outs and three KC Men on. . . what ELSE could go wrong. . .
Okay, Kid, just this inning. . . do your thing."

Duke and Jake return to the 'Dugout'. . .
Sammy rushes back to his position behind 'Home Plate'. . .
Sammy squats down into position and holds his Mitt in 'Strike Position'.

PITCHER'S MOUND: Raji goes through the entire routine again. He bends over at the waist and focuses like a laser, on the 'Strike Zone'.

Everything is blocked other the very center of Sammy's Catcher's Mitt, 'The Target'.

Raji continues to stare at the Zone.

DUGOUT: Duke is scowling, again. . .

"He's gonna drive me crazy! Put 'Sergio' in, Next Inning. . ."

Jake picks up the dugout phone. . .

"Mike, Yeah, . . . tell Sergio to warm-up for the Sixth. . .You Guys get him ready. . ."

PITCHER'S MOUND: Raji does his own version of the 'wind-up' and 'Pitches the Ball'. . .
It 'rockets past' the 'Batter', who lamely swings at it, nearly losing his balance. . .

Sammy smiles in satisfaction. There's even a slight smile on the UMP's face as he raises a fisted right. . . then loudly. . .

"Hike!"

DUGOUT: Duke's eyes are wide with disbelief. . . as he barks an order to Jake. . .
 "Find out how 'Fast' that BALL was?"

Jake makes a quick call on the 'Dugout' phone to their STAT Man . . . as Jake hangs up the phone, he has a big 'roundhouse' smile on his face.

"Eight-Five miles-per-hour, Duke!"

"Good GAWD. . . maybe he's got something. . ."

"He won't be able to keep that up, though."

"Right. . . 'Lucky Pitch'."

SERIES OF PITCHES: Fifth Inning. . . with two more incredibly fast pitches, the 'Top KC Batter' is 'Out'.

DUGOUT: Duke and Jake look at each other in true disbelief. . . as Jake adds. . .

"Three 'Lucky Pitches', Maybe?"

FIELD BOX AT THIRD: Ron and Fazal look around the COSCO Stadium to suddenly see more fans returning to their seats.
They both smile as Ron chuckles. . .

"Looks like, a lot of Fans are making U-turns."

HOME PLATE: The next batter gets a piece of Raji's 'Pitch', but the ball goes straight up vertical, and Sammy nabs it for another 'Out'.

DUGOUT: Duke and Jake now are astounded, as Jake yells out. . .

"That's 'Two Outs'. . .and there's still three KC Runners stranded on bases out there, Duke!"

But here comes their 'Top Batter' this Season, so far. . .

HOME PLATE: The KC Royal's 'Best Batter' swings and misses Raji's 'Fast Ball'.

BROADCAST BOOTH: From his lofty perch, Jim Rhodes, the A's All Season Announcer, and Ashton Ames, his 'color man', are peering down on the 'Game' and smiling broadly, as Rhodes starts his perspective. . .

"The Speed of this Kid's 'Pitch' is phenomenal!"

Ames jumps in, charged-up with excitement. . .

"You're telling me! His last Ball clocked in at '102 mph'."

Rhodes reacts, electrified. . .

"That's next to impossible, Ashton. . .what's going on here? . . ."

"Not sure that Raji, with his small stature, can keep it up that energy level much longer. . . Question is. . . Can he save the Inning, Jim? . . ."

PITCHER'S MOUND: Once again, Raji concentrates on his 'Target Spot' and throws one of his 'motion-stopping curve balls'. . .
The batter lamely chases it and misses it widely.

BROADCAST BOOTH: Rhodes and Ames describe the pitch, over deafening cheers from the Fans as The COSCO Stadium is now 'Standing Room ONLY.
Additional Fans waiting outside for the 6th Inning 'Freebee', have now been let in early, to watch the 'unexpected spectacle'. . .

Rhodes continues his crazy rant. . .

"Oh, my God! That 'Ball' seemed to stop in 'mid-air'!"

Ames chokes, as he unloads another comment. . .

"I swear, it made a left turn! It was unhittable!"

PITCHER'S MOUND: Raji pitches a 'Fast Curve', making the Batter swing and miss for the third strike.

The 'Batter', scowling, turns to Sammy and the UMP. . .as he spits it out. . .

"They're letting too many damned foreigners in!"

DUGOUT: Duke and Jake now are stunned. . .
As Duke adds. . .

"Oh My Gawd. . . He struck 'em all OUT!
He 'Stranded all three KC Runners' with a 'No
Hitter' Inning. . .what a 'Relief Pitcher', Damn
that 'Kid'!"

Jake piles on more accolades. . .

"I don't think it's Luck. . .That Kid's Got the
KNACK!"

"Cancel Sergio, Jake. . .This Kid's going, the last
Four Innings, unless he collapses, on that 'Damn
Mound'. . .

TIME JUMP: Raji goes on to give the Team a 'No-
Hitter' for the next Four Innings, driving the A's
to Rally and add Six Runs of their own, over the
course of the evening. . .

There is loud cheering throughout the park at
the End of the Ninth Inning, as a massive
Chinese fireworks display is launched above
COSCO STADIUM, as well as over the giant
Scoreboard Display which reads . . .

FINAL: Scoreboard - Ninth Inning. . .
Score - Kansas City Royals - 4 : Oakland A's - 6

As the fireworks display continues, and the
crowds continue their jubilance, Raji walks off
the 'Pitcher's Mound' heading for the COSCO
Stadium Locker Rooms.

He walks alone, but the other players glance at him, now 'very aware' of his presence. There is thunderous applause in the Stadium, which Raji seems to be oblivious to.

But a quick smile, comes to Raji's face when he spots Veena and Khaldoon and his other Pakistani Hindu friends in the Family Field Box waving and cheering him on. He also spots a group of young Pakistani Men in a nearby box, who he does not recognize.

Finally, Raji's focus falls on a beautiful, young raven-haired girl, Lalita, 22, who is sitting with the Pakistani Men. Raji' and Lalita's eyes lock for a moment.
At the same time, KESH, 28, an Indian Hindu seated in that same Box with the Pakistanis, notices Raji's eyes locked on Lalita.
KESH watches him very closely. . .

As Raji continues to walk, he glances across to the 'Third Base Field Box' where Ron and Fazal are now standing. They are cheering and applauding him and giving him the thumbs up. He tries to suppress his smile, but it's a losing battle.

As he approaches the stands, the spectators start standing, applauding and cheering wildly as he walks closer.

He stops and looks at the cheering fans, only then realizing that the adulation is for him.

Raji, his face stoic once again, yet he glances at all the happy, cheering people and in his modest and sincere manner, he bows his head to them, as he continues on to the Locker Rooms.
His humble gesture only draws more applause and adoration. . .

Chapter 13

The First Win 'Aftermath'

"I would look back later on that first save for the A's and realize how that night was a turning point and how it changed so many other things in my life."

LOCKER ROOM: In the COSCO Stadium Locker Room, Duke has the Oakland A's, Players and Coaches gathered around him. Everyone is excited and talking over one another.
When Raji, the last to enter, walks in everyone grows silent.

Raji walks to his locker and puts away his Glove, then grabs a towel to head for the showers.
Duke looks over at him and motions for him to join them. . .

"Raji. . . come over here and celebrate with us, please. . ."

Raji looks surprised to be invited. He walks over to the group, still standing a bit apart from the others, as he replies. . .

"Yes, Sir?"

"You did a 'Great Job', tonight, Kid."

Raji bows his head slightly.
Duke looks around at the other players.

"He did 'Great', didn't he, fellas!"

There are a few unintelligible responses that lack
any sign of enthusiasm.
Jake jumps in to fill the void. . .

"Glad you asked, to 'Take the Fifth Inning, Raji."

Awkward silence. Duke then adds his voice to
support the conversation. . .

"Well. . . what can we do for you, Raji? And what
do you want from me, specifically?"

"The chance someday to start a 'Game', Coach."

Now there is an 'audible grumbling' among the
other players. Especially the lead Pitchers. . .
Duke himself laughs uncomfortably.

"I'd say that's, way down the line."

He taps his temple. . .

"But it's here in the Old Bean, Raji. . .we need
you more, on the Relief Roster, for now. . .
But anyway. . . you did 'Great' and stood up to the
extreme 'Game' pressure."

"I'll try to do better, as the Season goes on, Coach."

Duke grins at his verbal humility. . .

"Now, that's the 'Spirit' I'm talking about, Raji"

But Jake reacts to Raji's comment, differently. . .

"Not sure how, you could do . . ."

Jake then pauses and looks around at the other Players. who are weighing his words. . .

". . . of course Raji, everyone can improve."

PARKING LOT – COSCO STADIUM:
It's late night after the Game when, the beautiful
Lalita and KESH are walking together toward a
high end sports sedan, exchanging words, as a
security beep sounds and the car starts.
KESH is concentrating on the events in the
Stadium from the Fifth Inning onward. His mind
is on Raji's miraculous and magical performance
against the KC Royals. He saved the entire Game
with his powers. . .as he jabs at Lalita. . .

"See, I was right. I knew when I heard about him
that 'Raji' is the one I seek. And this Game
Tonight proved it. All the signs are there. . .

I need to get to him, Lalita. To find a way to
'seduce' him. . . and after watching him observe
you. . . You, have become my 'seductress'. . ."

Lalita is obviously reluctant, as she reacts. . .

"But he seems like such. . ."

KESH instantly interrupts her. . .

"I've decided, he's the one I seek, Lalita. . .and
You, will be that vehicle to get my results. . ."

"But. . ."

"No 'buts', Lalita, you will do it!
. . . without objection, Case Closed!"

Lalita is clearly dismayed, as she turns her eyes away from the 'All Powerful' KESH.

They quickly enter KESH's car, as he gets behind the wheel. Lalita enters the car and sits uncomfortably in the front passenger seat near him. She is obediently 'silent' as they drive away.

"You have 'No Right' to challenge me, Lalita. The 'shame of your past' surely 'stings' at your cheek."

Again, Lalita averts her eyes, that are now brimming with tears, as she looks out her window into the black of night. She thinks back in 'Time' of how it got this way. . .his 'possession' and 'control' of her mind and soul. . .

LALITA'S FLASHBACK IN TIME: The Mumbai Nightclub that Lalita worked at. . .she is scantily dressed, dancing seductively in front of two Indian Businessmen. KESH is sitting nearby.

The First Businessman comments to his associate. . .

"She's a Hindu 'goddess'. . . look at those chiseled features on that face. . .
and that 'Body'. . ."

KESH enters their conversation. . .

"Lalita does look like a 'goddess', Gentlemen. . .
I should know. . ."

The Second Businessman is taken back in
surprise. . .

"Huh?"

KESH looks at him with his evil glowing eyes. . .

The Man reacts, then retreats. . .

"Nothing. . .I meant Nothing, please excuse me."

KESH looks at the First Businessman with the
same glowing eyes. . .as he questions. . .

". . .I believe you have something for me?"

The Businessman furtively hands KESH a rolled
up wad of money. . .

KESH counts the bills, then quietly to the Man. . .

"She'll be waiting for 'You', alone in your room."

"Will she agree to 'Service' us both?"

KESH smiles and 'nods' his agreement.

LATER: At an Upscale Hotel in Central Mumbai,
we see Lalita. It is late at night, almost dawn,
when she leaves the hotel. . .

Suddenly out of nowhere, KESH walks up to her and grabs her left arm.

"We're leaving in the morning, for Oakland in the USA. . ."

Lalita shocked. . .

"Oakland, California?! Why there?"

"I've secured a lucrative position with an IT Company there. . .for both of us. . .
But more important, Oakland is just where we need to be, where my objective plays his games of 'American Baseball'."

Lalita is dumbfounded as to why they must go. . .

"But, Why?"

KESH twists Lalita's arm a bit, making her cry out, as his 'Eyes' begin to 'glow' a reddish color.

"You need to learn 'NOT', to ask so many questions of me, Lalita."

LATER: KESH's swank Apartment North of Mumbai. . . Lalita is naked washing KESH's jet black hair. . .as she again asks. . .

"Why take me? You've got other girls."

"Because you're beautiful, smart, innocent. . .
And the right fit for a certain personality. . . I will
need all those talents for this very important
task."

Lalita sees that odd flash again in his reddening
eyes, like a 'Beast'.
She shakes her head to clear it. . .

Lalita focuses on the gold chain draped on
KESH's naked chest. Her eyes widen, as she
notices that a 'Talisman' with the 'Hindu God
Kali' is on the Medallion's Face. . .

She responds incredulously. . .fearful. . .

"The 'Medallion of Kali'! You're wearing it!
Kali is the 'God of Evil and Sin' and has been
banished by Vishnu. . .
Why do you wear such a vile symbol?"

KESH grabs Lalita's long black tresses and
viciously yanks. She moans in pain. He glares at
her with an evil menacing grin.

"I warned you "NOT' to ask, so many questions."

LALITA'S FLASHBACK ENDS:

Chapter 14

The Mysterious Lalita

"As I think back to this very moment in my life and the mysterious and beautiful Lalita, I realize there is something more to accomplishments, than material possessions and perpetual fame."

COSCO STADIUM – OAKLAND: Once again, another critical Game for Raji's evolution. This night the bright lights of COSCO Stadium seem to shine down on the luscious Green Playing Field, brighter than ever. . .

The Scoreboard Reads: Top of the Eighth Inning

NY Yankees - 7 : Oakland A's - 4

Raji is making the long walk from the 'Bullpen' as the Team's final designated 'Relief Pitcher', to hopefully save the next piece in their AL Pennant Race.

BROADCAST BOOTH:
Rhodes and Ames have been calling the Game all Night and are concerned for their prospects to Win against the Yankees. . .even with Raji. As Rhodes makes his usual announcement. . .

"Well, it's top of the Eighth, the Yankees ahead by Three runs. . . and Three Yankees on base and No Outs. . . It's Raji time, Folks!"

Ames chimes in with his added color. . .

"You're right. . . they're bringing in their 'Secret Weapon'. . .what I want to know is 'why on earth' don't they let Raji start.

Rhodes has his answer. . .

"That would probably cause a little indigestion, among their highly paid 'prima donna' first string 'Pitching Staff'. . ."

Ames retorts. . .

"But the kid has 'Saved Every Game', he's pitched. . . which is unprecedented in the entire American League this year!"

Rhodes makes his typical excuse. . .

"Maybe he just couldn't go the whole Nine yards, doesn't have the 'stamina' that it takes to 'Pitch an Entire Game'."

Ames backs down. . .

"I'll tell you one thing. . . as an 'A's Fan', he's a joy to watch!"

Rhodes, then adds his support. . .

"More than that. . .
He's taking us to the Play-Offs, this year. . .
. . . Let's watch a little bit of his 'Magic'."

PITCHING MOUND: Raji warms up, throwing a few balls back and forth with Sammy. He nods at Sammy indicating that he is ready to for his first pitch.

SERIES OF PITCHES: Raji does his now-famous focus on home plate and wind-up.
Everything except the 'Spot in Sammy's Mitt' is blocked from view.

In the Dugout, Duke and Jake seem to be calm and relaxed, as Duke quietly jokes to Jake. . .

"We could start to phone it in, from here on."

Jake laughs. . .

"Remember, when we worried about Raji taking too long."

"Gawd. . . The 'Kid' asked for an 'Inning' that day . . . Didn't know we were handing him the 'Entire Season'. . ."

On the Mound, Raji delivers a blistering strike that the Batter chases. . .

And then a slider that eludes the Batter and finally a curve that dips and turns, completely baffling the Batter. . .

Raji's 'Pitching results, 'Rallies the 'A's' Lineup' and they score Two more Runs in the Bottom of the Eighth, putting pressure on The Yankees. . .

Rhodes and Ames are calling the 'Final Batter' in the Top of the Ninth inning, as Raji goes through his ritual. . . Rhodes calls it. . .

"With a 1-2 Count, this could be the Yankee's Final out."

The Scoreboard Reads: Top of the Ninth Inning

NY Yankees - 7 : Oakland A's - 6

"With Frank Emerson up. . . the 'Yankee's Best Batter'. . . it's a 'Casey at the Bat' Scenario. And remember, Casey struck out. . .

They both watch in stunned disbelief, as Raji throws a 'Rocket' that nearly 'Burns the Air' itself'. . .

Emerson swings after the speedball, as it jets by at 'One-Hundred' even on the field radar screen.

Ames immediately injects his jest, for color. . .

"And so did 'Emerson'. . ."

Rhodes follows-up. . .

"That's the end of the 'Top'. . .
Now the A's have to score two more runs, and
we'll get 'Home Field' advantage for the AL
Pennant 'locked up'. . .

And so, they did it with a late Rally. . . outscoring
the Yankees. . .

Later, as Raji is walking off the field to
thunderous applause and cheers from the
packed COSCO Stadium. . .with the. . .

Final Scoreboard: Yankees 7   -   Oakland 8

And approaching the 'Private Field Boxes', he
again spots Lalita, who is standing at the railing
waiting for him. . .
But, KESH is right behind her, and his face is
'somber', as he focuses directly on Raji.

Lalita bends over the railing to Raji. . .

"Raji! Raji! Can I have your 'Autograph'?"

. . . She holds up a 'Program and a Pen' to him.

Raji smiles at the beautiful Lalita. . .

He then hands Lalita the Baseball, he's carrying.

"This is the 'Game Ball', I was just given by the 'Coach'. . . Meet me at the 'Player's Entrance Gate' and I'll sign the 'Ball and Your Programs' for you.
But I've got to go to the 'Lockers first and shower!
See you there. . ."

Lalita smiles, thrilled holding 'The Game Ball', as Raji exits the field.

KESH, grabs 'The Girl' around the waist from behind, with a vicious grip.

"Good job, Lalita. . .but be sure not to let this 'Wunderkind', charm the panties off You."

Lalita scowls, keeps her back to KESH and remains silent and unreactive. . .

Chapter 15

The Spoils of Seduction

"The mysterious and gorgeous 'Lalita', had suddenly captivated my mind and unfortunately, my 'Mortal Soul', with an inexplicable 'Power'. At once, I was drawn into her 'Dream-World' without full control of my own faculties."

OUTSIDE COSCO STADIUM – OAKLAND:
The Players Entrance Gate – Late Night. . .
Lalita has a big smile on her face, as she clutches 'The Game Ball' while waiting for Raji to arrive and sign it. . .
Other Players are exiting, as more than several, give the stunning Lalita a second and even a third look. . .
While, Lalita pans them, craning her neck, looking 'only' for Raji. . .
When she spots him, she beams at him and holds the 'Game Ball' high in the air. . .
Raji instantly hurries over to her, followed by a trail of 'Sports Reporters'. . . one of which gives Lalita the once over. . .before addressing Raji!

"Is this your 'Girlfriend', Raji?"

Raji's face turns 'Seven-Shades of Red', while Lalita smiles beautifully, at the question.

But she glares, at the Sports Reporter, who's gaze seems focused on her cleavage, exposed by the deep 'V' plunge of her blouse, as he gets her answer. . .

"I'm afraid I'm not that 'Lucky'."

Raji is surprised by her answer, as he remarks.

"It would not be You, who would be the 'Lucky One', Lalita."

The Sports Reporter decides to play along. . .

"Might I add. . .
That you would 'Both be Lucky'. . .for very different reasons. . ."

Lalita, then turns to the reporter again, with a stern face. . .

"Can you give us some 'Privacy', please, Sir?"

She then grasps Raji's hand gently, leading him away, from the growing flock of News 'Hounds'.

Raji smiles, glowing at her confidence. . .

"So that's how it's 'Done'. I always have trouble getting away from the 'Press', Lalita."

"That is how it's 'Done', Raji. . .just follow my lead. . ."

"I think, it's your 'Pretty Face' that had a lot to do with it."

They both laugh, smiling at each other. . .

LATER THAT NIGHT: At a nearby Coffee Shop, Raji's signed 'Baseball' is laying on the table where Lalita is sitting. . .
As Raji walks over, with two hot coffees. . .
setting them down on the table, and speaking. . .

"I noticed you before. . . at the 'Home Games'."

"I've been to quite a few, lately. . . I usually come with my Company Co-workers. I'm a Network Specialist. . .
I've been hoping that you'd notice me."

"I think every man, who has eyes and can see, has 'Noticed You', Lalita."

Raji's face reddens, uncontrollably. . .

"Please, Lalita, I meant no disrespect, by that."

"You are such a nice man, Raji. . ."

Lalita's face saddens, her smile fades, a little.

"There are so 'Many Men'. . . out there, who are NOT so nice."

Raji 'nods', acknowledging her feelings, then quickly changes the subject. . .

"Lalita, I do not mean to be presumptuous, but I hope we can begin seeing, one another. Nothing would please me more. . ."

"Actually, I was hoping you felt, as I did, too. . . Raji. . . there's a 'Special Spark', between us."

Raji smiles, as he gazes at the exquisite, Lalita.

Within an hour, they have parted ways. . . with each returning to their own Apartments, for the night. . .

THE BEDROOM OF KESH'S APARTMENT:

The Next morning KESH is up and holding the 'Autographed Game Ball' with an evil sneer on his face. . .
Lalita seems to sense what is going to happen, as she appears upset, and averts her eyes away from his wicked scowl. . .

"Look at this 'Ball', Lalita!"

KESH clasps Lalita's face, then yanks her forward, forcing her to look at the 'Ball'.

"This is what you think is 'The Spoils of Your Seduction', HAH! This is NOTHING. . .
I have told you, what I need. . .
You are expected to obtain that 'Object' and bring it to ME, this very night."

Lalita is broken, as she weakly replies. . .

"How will I know, 'IT'?
. . . How will I even recognize, 'IT'?"

"It will, at that 'MOMENT' of awareness. . .
Become obvious to You. And I warn you, don't FAIL ME, Lalita."

Lalita sighs, with tears running down her face, as KESH storms off, and instantly disappears.

ONE WEEK LATER: Kauffman Stadium – Kansas City. . .
The Kansas City Royals are leading in this 'Division Playoff', with the score 'Two Games' to the 'A's One', as they take the Field in the Bottom of the Eighth, against the starting Batter for the A's, at the plate.

Scoreboard: ROYALS 10 : Oakland 'A's 9

In the A's Bullpen, Raji and Sergio are sitting in their usual spot, a distance away from the other relief pitchers, as Sergio supports his friend. . .

"This is a proud moment for the A's and especially for you, Raji. 'You got us here'. . . the First DIVISION Playoff Game, in over Forty-Years . . .and we're the 'HOME TEAM'.

If we Win tonight, we go 'HOME' for the 'Final Game of This Division' . . . Then start, the Championship Series. . .
Who do you think we'll face?"

Raji doesn't think, somehow he knows. . .

"For sure, it will be the Toronto Blue Jays. . .
But in answer to your statement, Sergio. . .
It's the 'Batter's Rallies and Teamwork', that 'really got us here' and of course, some other unusual events, that may have 'gotten me here'."

"You are always a mystery, Raji. . ."

Sergio pauses, as he watches the A's 'fly out' after tying the Game. . .

Scoreboard: ROYALS 10 : Oakland 'A's 10

"How's it going with the 'Beautiful', Lalita?"

Raji smiles, as the A's take the Field and the Bullpen Phone rings. . .

"I'm completely enchanted with Lalita, Sergio. . . I hope to build a future with her. . ."

'The Senior Relief Pitcher' yell's to Raji, as Sergio finishes. . .

"I have no doubt that you will. Everything just seems to go your way, Raji."

In minutes, Raji enters the 'Pitcher's Mound' in the 'Top of the Ninth and pulls another. . . 'No-Hitter', as the 'A's add another run, in the Bottom of the Ninth, sending the Division Final back to Oakland. . .

Final Score: ROYALS 10 : Oakland 'A's 11

COSCO STADIUM: Another Night Game for the Division Final, with the A's Batters taking the lead, as Raji throws Game Winning 'No-Hitters' from the Fourth to the Ninth Inning . . .

Final Score: ROYALS 0 : Oakland 'A's 6

The Royals fans are shocked, after losing the Division Title, while Oakland A's fans are jubilant, including Ron, Fazal, Veena, Khaldoon, and the Pakistani Fans, including Lalita.

Announcer Rhodes finishes his commentary. . .

"Well, another 'Win' for the A's and another monumental save for 'Raji Swat', as we 'Win the Division', for the First Time in 21st Century Baseball History!"

Ames comes back with his perspective. . .

"This kid has a real chance of being MVP of the 'Division Playoffs'. . . that's quite an unusual honor for a 'Relief Pitcher. . ."

"But well-deserved, Ames! I think I can safely say, that the Oakland A's, probably wouldn't be here, if it wasn't for their 'Star Relief Pitcher'."

As Raji walks off, he locks eyes with his precious 'Lalita', who waves to him enchantingly.

Lalita calls out loudly, to Raji. . .

"I'll meet you, at Your Place."

Raji smiles in return, as he quickly disappears into the 'Team's Locker Rooms'. . .

THE APARTMENT: Raji's Master Bedroom –
That night, Raji and Lalita lie together naked in the darkened bedroom. They have just made love and Raji holds Lalita tightly. . .

"You know, I really need you, Lalita. . .
I have many challenges ahead, and I need to feel that you will be there for me, during each of them. . ."

Lalita averts her eyes, that are now brimming, in what only she knows, are 'regretful tears'.

"Raji, it seems that all you really need, is your 'Great Talent'."

"My 'Talent' is nothing without Love. Your Love."

He seems to drift off, into a Dream-World. . .

"Next, we will face the 'Blue Jays' for the 'American League Championship'.
It's funny. . .
I know, it's 'my mouth', that forms those words, but, I am still in disbelief, as to where I actually find myself. . .I'm 'Not' in the Swat Valley anymore. . .I'm almost in, another Dimension."

Lalita glows at Raji.

"You have earned it, Raji. . .
And you'll always do fine, you'll be a Winner. . .
a Big Winner. . .
So, if . . . If ever, I must be away, you will still be
in my heart that way."

Raji holds Lalita even tighter, knowing
something is brewing. . .

"I hope, I will 'never' have to learn that lesson,
with you away from me. . ."

Lalita lowers her eyes in dismay, as a tear traces
down her cheek. . .

Much later that night, Raji and Lalita are still in
bed together in the pitch dark room. . .
As suddenly Lalita sits up. The bedside clock
indicates 3:10 A.M . . .
Lalita peers at Raji, who is solidly asleep.
She carefully moves around the room, then
quietly opens his night stand drawer, looks
inside then closes it. . .

Next, Lalita opens Raji's walk-in closet and looks
around it, opening a few boxes and searching
behind the hanging clothes. . .
She sighs, frustrated, then silently walks back
toward the bed. . . noticing a 'slight blue glow' in
the bottom drawer of Raji's main chest. . .

Like a ghost, she squats down and opens the
drawer. . . then gasps, almost too loud, as she
checks Raji's face. . . but he's still 'fast asleep'.

It's there. . .a faintly shimmering 'beat-up old
leather Cricket Ball'. . . it's aglow in 'neon blue'.

Lalita makes one more glance over at Raji. . .
Then grabs the 'Ball', stuffing it into her tote bag.

Quickly, she grabs her clothes off the floor by the
bed and moves through the doorway naked. . .to
avoid detection, while hurriedly dressing in the
Living Room. . .
Spotting a message pad & pen by the door, she
writes a short note and lays it on the table,
partially under a bronze 'Cricket Trophy'. . .
In moments, she disappears out of the room,
into a foggy 'Oakland' night. . .

Several hours later, Raji wakes and stumbles
into his bathroom. . .
Upon returning, he realizes, Lalita is gone. . .

His mid is racing, as he rushes around the
apartment searching for her, but silently
knowing, there is something odd going on. . .

Finally, at the front doorway, he spies her note
under his bronze 'Cricketer', grabs it, scans it,
then hurries back into the bedroom. . .

Then opening his main 'Chest-of-Draws'. . . he screams out. . .

"Lalita. . .what have you done to me!"

He re-reads her note in wild panic. . .

'Raji, please forgive me. . . I have betrayed you. Know that 'I do love you'. Please don't try to find me. . .Lalita. . .'

Raji is devastated, tears brim in his eyes. . .
He again rummages frantically, all around the drawers. Then sits on the bed. . .wide awake now, fathoming just what the 'Loss' of his 'Talisman', Hanuman's transformed 'Blue Neon Cricket Ball' means. . .
He hangs his head over the empty drawer, crumples Lalita's note and quietly sobs in his ultimate anguish. . . 'His Good Fortune is Over'!

Again, he cries out. . .in tormented pain. . .

"Lalita. . .you've 'Destroyed Me'!"

Chapter 16

The Ultimate Betrayal

KESH'S APARTMENT – DAY:
KESH is gloating, as he holds the battered old ‘Cricket Ball’ shimmering in ‘Neon Blue’ light. . .

Lalita is sitting on the couch, her eyes bloodshot from crying. . . as KESH recites his admonition, of his Ancient Foe. . .

“This ‘Ball’ contains the powers that ‘Hanuman’ possessed. But he foolishly gave it away, to save his ‘Avatar’ in the ‘Battle of the Hindu Temple’ in ‘The Swat Valley’. . .
Now that ‘Power’ is mine alone, and I shall take my rightful seat, next to ‘Vishnu’.”

Lalita is stunned as she hears this. She looks at KESH with new eyes. . . informed eyes, but fearful. . .terrified. . .
Breathing heavily, she stares at him. . .

“Who. . . Who are you?!”

KESH's eyes, turn a ‘Deep Red’, as he beams at Lalita. . .

“I think by now. . . You know who I am!”

A look, of serious realization fills, Lalita's face.

"The Medallion! The Medallion you wear. . . constantly. . ."

"That Medallion, is the 'Medallion of the God Kali', Lalita. . .
. . . For that is. . .WHO I AM!"

The room shakes from KESH's booming voice. His eyes flash in hues of 'Yellow, then Red Neon'.

Lalita must cover her ears, as she shrinks from the 'Intensity and Heat' of KESH's gaze.

Lalita is trembling and shaken to her core. . . but stands defiantly. . . facing him!

"Do what you will, with Me . . . I accept that I am a cheat, a liar and a whore. . .But what happens to Raji?"

"Raji will return to what he's been all along. . . just an ordinary 'Pakistani Boy' from the 'Swat Valley'. . .with absolutely, NO FUTURE!"

His evil smirk, chills her to her inner 'Soul'. . .

"But Raji has one 'Last Important Role', yet to play. He will draw the others into my ultimate ambush. . ."

"The others? Who are the others?"

KESH raises both arms, then casts Lalita downward. . . crashing to the floor.

"You never learn, Lalita. You always ask, 'Too Many Questions'. . ."

Broken and physically weakened, she tentatively tries to reason with him. . .

"You have, what you 'Wanted'. . . You have, 'The Ball'. . . It's 'The Talisman' you desired. . . Why is that, not enough?!"

". . . 'The Ball' is ONLY, but a 'Token' for my Triumph'. . .

I will need 'Complete and Absolute Victory'. . .

. . . As for you, Lalita, your usefulness has run its course. I will summon my 'Army of Guardians', who will send you, on your way. . ."

"Back to Mumbai?"

KESH again, glares at Lalita, for a brief moment.

"In a sense, that may be the best retribution, for your disloyalty. . . a 'Lifetime of Whoring', until your 'Beauty' is withered completely away. . ."

ROGERS CENTRE - TORONTO, CANADA:

It's 'two weeks later' and both ALCS Teams are set, with 'The Toronto Blue Jays' gaining 'Home Team Advantage' for the Championship. . .

It's the First Game of a Seven Game Series and The Blue Jays have taken the field. The first batter for the Oakland A's is up.

While inside the Bullpen of the Oakland A's. . . a glum looking Raji Swat is sitting at the end of the bench with his fellow 'Relief Pitcher' Sergio. Sergio looks at Raji with serious concerns. . .

"You okay, Man?"

"I've lost everything, Sergio."

Sergio looks concerned, as he tries to sort it out.

"Whatever do you mean, Raji?"

"Lalita has left me. I don't know where she is!"

"Why did she leave?"

"I don't know. She doesn't want me to find her. . . . And now, I have lost my ability to 'Pitch'."

"That cannot be true, Raji!

I can believe that the 'Girl' is gone, but not your incredible 'Talent'. . .You are just feeling down."

"No, Sergio. That 'Gift is Gone'. . . physically 'Gone'. . . 'Gone Forever'. . .
 . . . until she returns my. . .uh. . ."

Raji stops in mid-sentence, to 'Not Reveal' the vital secret of his 'Powers'. . .

Sergio is stunned as he looks at his friend with disbelief. . .

TIME JUMP: It's finally the Bottom of the Eighth Inning and the Manager and Coaches of the A's need the 'Miracle Man'. . .

The scoreboard reads: Oakland 3 - Blue Jays - 5

The Relief Pitchers clap, as Raji enters the Playing Field to the cheers of the few Oakland Fans seated near the Dugout. . .

Raji walks across the perfectly manicured Field toward the 'Pitcher's Mound'.
Raji is being enthusiastically cheered, by some Blue Jay fans as well. . .

The 'Blue Jay's announcer even gives him a positive intro, as he reaches the Mound. . .

"It's the 'Bottom' of the 8th and here comes Oakland's Mr. Fixit. . .Let's see what he can do to get them back in this Game, today. . .
The announcer's 'Color Guy', then adds his thoughts. . .

"It's amazing. . . this Guy has come out of 'Nowhere this Season' and he's got Fans on both sides cheering him on, out there.

All we can say is, it looks like 'Raji Swat' is on his way to becoming 'One of the Greats'. . . a true 'Baseball Hero'!"

At long last, Raji does his unique wind-up and stares into home plate. But Raji sees everything just as it is, as everyone else does. . .

He clearly sees the UMP, the Catcher and the Batter. . .'No Focus'. . .No Target'. . .

Raji looks at Sammy's 'Mitt', that he holds above the plate. Sammy's 'Mitt', is no longer the 'only thing' that is visible to Raji. . .

Raji throws his 'First Pitch', with all his might. He throws a . . .

UMP (shouts loudly) . . .

"Ball!"

There's an audible 'GASP' heard from the
'Oakland Fans', throughout the Stadium.

At Home Plate. . . Sammy stands, to throw the
ball back to Raji. . .as he remarks to the UMP. . .

"Did You say, 'BALL'?"

UMP. . . "Ball" . . .

In the Dugout, Duke chokes on his gum and
looks at Jake. . .

"Ball?!"

Jake shrugs. . .

"Ball. . . Boss!"

In the Oakland Field Box, near Third Base,
Ron and Fazal are dumbfounded. . .
looking at each other. . .as Ron repeats it.

"Ball. . .?"

Fazal, then comes in with a quick excuse. . .

"He's just off focus, a little, Ron. . .
you know off his 'Center Target'."

In the stands, at a Family 'Field Box'. . .
Khaldoon's surprised look, catches Veena off
guard, as she's ordering drinks. . .

"Mama, Raji just threw 'a Ball'."

Veena retorts, without even looking at the field.

"He'll throw a 'Strike', Next."

At a Specialty 'Field Box' in the stands behind Home Plate. . . KESH, smiling and animated, is now standing in the center of the Pakistani Fans, who look dazed and confused. Happily, he 'Boos' loudly, nodding to his companions who, zombie-like, stand and 'Boo' along with him. . .

In the Broadcast Booth both Announcers are jubilant. . . as they were holding their breath, expecting a sizzling 'Fast Ball Strike'. . .
The Color Guy adds. . .

"I don't think 'Raji Swat' has thrown a Ball in the past 'Ten Games' as a 'Relief Pitcher' . . ."

The Jay's Announcer corrects him. . .

"He's NEVER thrown one in 'Regular Season Play'. . . He's been 'Super-Human', that's what really scares me. . ."

Out at the Pitcher's Mound, Raji is wincing and holding his arm in pain.

Finally, he catches the 'Ball' back from Sammy and begins his ritual again. . .

The wind up, the aim. . . but there's 'No Neon Blue Color' blocking everything out. His 'Target' is not defined. . .
He pitches. . . and it's. . . another 'Ball'.

In the Dugout. . . Duke is taking a swig of water and blows it out, after the 'Second Ball'.

Jake, spits out his comment to Duke. . .

"It's a fluke. . ."

Back in the Oakland Field Box near Third Base, Ron and Fazal, continue to be confused by Raji's Pitching problem . . .

"Another 'Ball', Ron. . .not sure what's wrong?"

"I thought I was hearing things, Fazal."

At the Family 'Field Box'. . .Khaldoon looks at her Mother, as Veena maintains her cool. . .

"He'll get a 'Strike' call. . . He's a clever boy. He's tricking them, Khaldoon."

In KESH's Specialty 'Field Box', he's on his feet applauding and laughing, motioning for the others to join him. They stand and mimic KESH's behavior.

At the Mound, Raji again does his best to focus, winds up then pitches. . .

The UMP calls it. . . it's 'Ball Three'. . . the UMP stands and resets for the next pitch.

In the Dugout, Duke is red-faced with a look of disbelief. He's reeling, as Jake has to steady him.

At Home Plate, Sammy looks up at the UMP and 'Calls Time Out'. . .

Raji is clutching his arm. Sammy runs out to the 'Mound', where he is joined by Duke and Jake.

Duke starts first. . .

"What's wrong kid? You pull something? Your elbow?"

"I pulled my arm out, because I'm not that strong. . ."

"What do you mean, you're not that 'Strong'?"

"I'm a fraud. I am 'Not' a natural."

Duke chokes it back. . .

"One 'Hell'uva' time to tell us."

Jake jumps into the melee. . .

"What do you 'Mean', Raji?"

"I lost my ability to 'Target and Pitch'. . . I've lost
my 'Power and Speed'. . .
I've lost everything. . .

Tears begin to form in Raji's eyes. . .

"And . . . I've lost my 'Girlfriend' and . . ."

Duke explodes with the answer. . .

"That's it. He's upset over a 'Broad'. . .
Look Kid. Pretty young women get old and outta
shape."

Jake and Sammy give Duke an incredulous look.
Duke redirects to Jake and Sammy. . .

"So kill me, Boys, I'm trying. . .

Raji, you'll have your Baseball Career forever,
your 'Great Record' to look back on when you're
old and gray. . .
They'll be plenty of 'women' along the way."

Raji reacts. . .trying to salvage the argument. . .

"You don't understand. . .Duke"

"Raji, you young 'Kids' don't think us old
buzzards understand, but we went through the
same things. . ."

Jake gets serious. . .specific. . .

"You got any 'Arm' left, Kid?"

"It hurts, and 'No', I don't have any 'Arm' left, but I wouldn't, even if it didn't hurt, this 'bad'."

Raji hangs his head.

Duke, 'stage whispers', to Jake. . .

"The kid's 'crack in' up."

Jake answers back in an undertone . . .

"You need to take him out, now."

Duke, again whispers', to Jake. . .

"Christ. . . there goes the 'Freak'in Series'."

He looks disgusted, at Jake. . .

"Call up, Sergio."

Jake trots back to the dugout.

Raji and Duke start to walk off the 'Mound'. . .
There's a 'MOAN' of disbelief that echoes
throughout the Stadium. . .
Sammy returns to Home Plate. . .

The Announcers, yell out to their listeners. . .

"Oh, my GAWD. Raji is out! . . . Looks like an injury. . . this could flip the Game to the Jays!

. . .We hope for his sake, whatever it is, heals up without surgery. . ."

Down on the Field. . . Raji walks toward the locker room. . . Duke back to the Dugout. . . There's a buzz all around the Stadium.
. . . As he nears the Stands, many of his Fans are on their feet giving Raji a Standing Ovation.

When he gets to the entrance, a Trainer comes out to escort him, as Raji looks at The Field Box where Lalita used to sit, but she's not there.

Only KESH is there, looking directly at him. . .
KESH laughs in his face. . .
The Trainer provides lift support, as Raji makes his way, into the locker rooms. . .

Chapter 17

The Dream Sequence

TORONTO HOTEL ROOM – NIGHT: Raji lies awake in his Suite, tossing and turning. He's saddened when he turns and looks at the empty pillow lying next to him, as he thinks of Lalita and what she has done to him. . .
'Where did she go. . .
And Why did she steal 'The Talisman' . . .'

After several hours, Raji finally drifts off to sleep. But it is a fitful sleep. . .
He frowns, balls up and begins to moan. . .

Suddenly, he's in a deep 'Dream State', as he begins mumbling, unconscious thoughts. . .

'Where... where is it?!'

A 'Dream Sequence' begins, as he goes even deeper, into a cloud filled imaginary world. . .
He's walking across what seems to be an endless verdant green baseball field. . . looking all around for something.

'I can't find it! Where is it?'

Unexpectedly, two ghostly figures appear before him. One of the figures is 'Major Kahmal' the other is an unknown very powerful 'Entity'.

Uncontrollably, Tears begin spilling out of Raji's eyes. He runs and falls on his knees at the feet of Kahmal, as he implores his help. . .

'Master Kahmal, I need you so. Everything is lost!'

Instantly, Master Kahmal appears in A powerful mystical form, with a bejeweled white robe. . . then speaks to Raji. . .

'Nothing is lost, that can't be found.'

Raji cries his response. . .

'The GIFT that I received from 'Hanuman' has been stolen. I look for it even now, but it is nowhere to be found.'

At that moment, the powerful entity transforms and appears again, it's actually the 'GOD HANUMAN', as he steps forward onto their Mortal plane. . .

'Raji, it is me, Hanuman. . .'

Raji's eyes are wide in astonishment. He bows in front of the powerful 'God Hanuman'. . .and speaks a prayer. . .

'My praise to you, Honored One.'

'Once, You came to MY rescue, Raji and now I come to Yours.'

'Will you help me find the 'Talisman'. . . 'The Blue Neon lighted Cricket Ball', so I may again, restore my 'super-mortal' powers. . . Oh Great, Hanuman?'

'It was always within You, it will always be You, Raji. . . It is ONLY YOU, who will rediscover what is missing, Yet I gave it to YOU, as a blessing in My 'Swat Valley Shrine' that day, so long ago. . .

'I don't understand, Oh Holy One. . .'

'Soon, you will be challenged like never before and face difficulties. . . That may seem insurmountable. . . but in the end, YOU will succeed. . .'

'I have faith in YOU, Oh Great One. . . and in Master Kahmal, that I shall achieve this Success. . . but I still do not know how. . . without my 'Talisman'. . .'

'Ahhh. . . but you must ALSO, have faith in Yourself. . .'

Silently and mystically. . . all the images of 'Master Kahmal' and 'The God Hanuman', begin to slowly fade from Raji's 'Dreamworld'. . .

As, Master Kahmal, his voice growing faint, disappears at last. . .

'Look for us, Raji . . . Look for us. . .'

Raji's mind rushes, 'like a surfacing submarine'. To the upper shallows of reality. . .

Incredulously, he yells out as he enters. . . full mental cognizance. . .

"Look for you?! Where? When?"

Raji desperately tries to get his answer. . . To return to the 'Dream Scape World'. . .

"Stay! Don't go!"

But it's too late, as. . . 'The Dream and The images' completely disappear. . .the 'Voices' are silenced. There are tears in Raji's eyes. . .

"Master Kahmal. . . Oh Great 'God Hanuman'!"

Realizing he's lost that moment. . . he awakes
with a start, looking all around the room. He
sighs, devastated and bewildered. . .
Raji, at last completely conscious, hangs his head
in depression. . .

Chapter 18

The World Series – 2034

COSCO STADIUM - OAKLAND, CALIFORNIA:

It was only by a last Inning 'Home Run' in the final Game of the ACLS Series by the 'Oakland A's' that they Won the best of 'Seven Games' against 'The Toronto Blue Jays'. . . thus gaining 'Home Team Advantage' for the 'World Series'. . .

It's two weeks later and 'The Entire Oakland A's Team and Coaches' are standing in a line on the perfectly manicured COSCO Stadium Playing Field. . .
Rhodes and Ames are announcing the 'First Home Game' of the 2034 World Series. . .

"Let's hear it for your ACLS Championship A's."

There is thunderous Applause, Cheers and massive Chinese Fireworks Displays' across the evening sky around the Stadium. . .
as the players file off toward the 'A's' dugout.

For the first time since his injury. . .
Raji is in Full uniform, but not playing.

Rhodes and Ames begin their usual banter and cajoling, before announcing the Game's 'Play by Play'. . .

"Excitement is in the air, Folks. The Oakland A's have finally made it to the 2034 World Series. . . 'Even', without their 'Star Relief Pitcher'. . . 'Raji Swat'."

Ames quickly jumps in, to blunt Rhodes comment, just a bit. . .

"Well, let's face it, they squeaked by a very toughly contested ALCS Series against 'The Blue Jays. . .going the full 'Seven Games'. . .
And now, they're up against 'The LA Dodgers', who are 'even more' heavily favored to take the World Series. . . in Only 'Four Straight Games'!"

A SECRET GAMBLING ROOM - LAS VEGAS, NV:

Rob Jerome, 38, and Gino Capito, 42, are working at a 'Mob Gambling' Conference Table with ten other operatives, as they are both fixed on their Laptop Network Screens. . .

While intensely listening to. . .

Rhodes and Ames, calling the 'World Series' in Oakland, California. . .

COSCO STADIUM - OAKLAND, CALIFORNIA:

"As you have said, Ames. . .The 'Odds Makers' in VEGAS have the 'Dodgers' in Four. . .but I think that's pathetic. . .Just because Raji's . . ."

"Right, Rhodes, in 'Four'. . . unless 'Raji' makes it back into Play, once again. . ."

"Well, Let's keep our fingers crossed, A's Fans!
. . . And anything else we can 'Cross'. . .
Gawd knows, we need 'Raji', to 'Seal Their Fate'!"

A SECRET GAMBLING ROOM - LAS VEGAS, NV:

Rob Jerome stops working his Laptop 'Sports Book' and glances over to Gino. . .

"You hear all that, Bubbie?"

"Of Course, Robbie! You know how much we stand to lose, if this 'Kid' does, make a come-back?!"

"Yeah, I know. That's why I have a terminal case of indigestion. . .

"Close to $800 Million. . . "

"We'd be 'Dead' Financially and Physically!"

"You know, Bubbie. . . this 'Paki Kid' couldn't have lost 'The Talent', he's had 'All Season'. . ."

"I, know. . . It's impossible."

"It has to be a ploy, Robbie. . . A gambit. . .
Somebody's wanting to undermined us. . .
And make a ton of money to our detriment."

"Yeah, if he comes back, we're screwed."

"Just think, anybody betting on the A's right now could clean up. . .
If, the 'Paki'. . .makes a come-back. . .
Then. . . Suddenly. . ."

Gino makes 'air quotes' around 'Suddenly'. . .
as Rob finishes. . .

". . . Recovers."

"Hey, we gotta send our 'Wise Guys' out and make sure this Kid doesn't recuperate. . .
too quickly . . ."

Rob 'nods' his head, in agreement, as they both share an intense look. . .

"We don't want the 'Kid' taken out. . .just roughed up and 'Out of Commission' for the Series."

"Hell, Yeah, Gino. . . we want him around for the 'Next Season', for sure. He does crazy things to the odds."

The two 'Mob Bookies', share a chuckle. . .

TIME JUMP: It's Game Two of the World Series and the 'LA Dodgers'. are ahead by 'One Game' winning the previous Night. . .

'First' Game Score: Oakland 2 - Dodgers - 5

COSCO STADIUM - OAKLAND, CALIFORNIA:

The Night Lighting seems more intense than ever as Raji trots over to the Bullpen. . . glancing up to 'The Family Field Box', where his Mother and Sister always sit. . .

But for some unexplained reason, they are not there. Raji is really bewildered. . .

In the 'Bullpen'. . . Raji sits by himself, at the end of the bench, once again, isolated from the other players. . .
Unexpected, out of nowhere. . . Duke walks up to him. . .

"How's the arm?"

"Still sore, Coach."

"Did they keep it iced up, for you, tonight?"

"It doesn't help."

"Wonderful. . .
Maybe tomorrow's, 'Day Game in LA', huh?"

Raji shrugs. Duke rolls his eyes. Martin, another 'Relief Pitcher', overhears the exchange.

"I told you, I lost it, Coach."

'Relief Pitcher' Martin spews his crap. . .

"We told You, 'he Never had it', Coach."

"Shut up, Martin. You Never had, what he had, even for a day. . ."

In the Stadium Front Row, Left of First Base, Two 'Wise Guy's, Rik, 32, and Johnny, 35, are wearing 'LA Dodger' hats and T-shirts. Their faces are decorated in 'Dodger Blue and White' face paint.
They're standing. . .but they aren't watching the Game. . . they're watching Raji, down in the A's Bullpen.

Later, after 'Several Innings', at a 'Long Ad Break'. . .We see Raji looking downcast. . . he's not even watching the Game, when Ron accompanied by Duke, walks up to him. . .
They both, look concerned. . .as Ron opens up. . .

"We need to talk to you, Raji."

Duke emphasizes it, a bit more. . .

"Let's take it back, in the Locker Room."

As they enter the Lockers. . .
Raji looks worried. . . he looks back and forth at
Ron and Duke.

"What's wrong? Am I fired. . .
 I wouldn't blame you. . ."

Duke puts him at ease. . .

"You're not fired, 'Kid'. . ."

Duke looks at Ron, who pulls Raji down on the
bench and sits next to him.

The Stadium Manager just got a call, from. . .
someone, who claims that your Mother and
Sister, have been kidnapped. . ."

Raji leaps to his feet. . . His eyes are wide in
panic. . .

"I didn't see them in the Stands, and now I know
why. . .
Kidnapped?!
Is it a prank. . .Ron, what's up!"

"Security checked it out. It's NOT a prank. There were witnesses to their abduction. . ."

"Who would do this?
Why would anyone take them . . .What do they want?!
Is this a Ransom. . .
We've got to find them. . ."

"All unknowns for now, Raji. The Cops are on their way here. . ."

Raji plops back down on the bench. He holds his head, tears streaking down his face. . .

"It's all my fault. Had I remained a 'Normal Boy' in the Swat Valley, without these big crazy dreams, none of this would have happened."

Ron sighs and looks at Duke. . .

"We'll find your Mom and Sister, 'Kid'. . .
And . . . we'll get the 'Bastards' who took them."

Out in the COSCO Stadium, in his 'Special Field Box', KESH and his fellow Pakistanis, who are now his 'Private Minions', are animated, cheering on the Dodgers. . .

While coming down the steps, nearby, is an innocuous 'Peanut Vendor', his uniform cap tilted downward, nearly covering one eye. . .

KESH sees him and yells out to the vendor. . .

"Hey, Peanut Man! Toss me, One 'Bag'!"

The 'Vendor' throws the bag of peanuts right at
KESH, but it's not a 'Normal Toss'. . .
The throw is so 'fast and powerful', that the 'Bag'
is steaming, when KESH tries to catch it. . .
It's so 'Hot', he's forced to drop it to the ground.

KESH whispers to himself. . .grinning. . .

'They're here...'

KESH slyly growls, as he turns and faces the
vendor directly on. . .

The 'Vendor' also grins, at KESH. . .

"The 'Peanuts' are on me, Sir."

The 'Vendor' pushes his cap back revealing that
it's 'The Hindu God Hanuman', whose eyes flash
'Neon Blue' for an instant. . .
ONLY KESH can see the 'Powerful Challenge'.

KESH to himself. . .

'The War has commenced. . .
. . . the Final Battle is engaged. . .'

TIME JUMP: By this time at Night, Game Two of the World Series is OVER, and once again the 'LA Dodgers' have Won. They're now ahead by 'Two Games' and the Series moves to LA, tomorrow. . .

'Second' Game Score: Oakland 6 - Dodgers - 7

At the same time, inside 'The A's Locker Room', Uniformed Cops and plainclothes Detectives surround Raji, who is sitting on the bench next to Ron.

The Older Detective, speaks first. . .

"You have any 'Enemies', Raji?"

"Everyone on my 'Team', except 'Sammy and Sergio' and . . . maybe the Coaches."

"Why's, that?"

Ron immediately jumps in . . .

"They hate him, because they consider him an outsider, and he's a better Player than they are."

The Older Detective adds. . .

"Professional jealously?"

Ron 'nods' his agreement. . .

The Junior Detective, then squeezes in . . .

"We've reviewed the 'Surveillance Videos'. Your Mom and Sister made it into COSCO Stadium. . . But we didn't find any 'Videos', of them leaving."

Raji perks up. . . *'maybe that's good news'*. . .

"So they're here. . .
. . . Still here, in the Stadium?!"

"We have combed every inch. But can't find any trace of them. . .
Don't worry. . . Our Guys, are still searching."

"Please find them, Detective."

"That's the plan, Mr. Swat."

Raji sighs, then lowers his eyes. . .
Speaking softly, almost to himself. . .

"I shall, then, look for them myself. . ."

Chapter 19

The Final Battle

INNER HALLWAYS - COSCO STADIUM:

Raji is walking down a dimly lit hallway. He is opening and looking in doors, as he makes his way down the hall.

Unrealized, and following a distance behind him are the 'Wise Guys', Rik and Johnny. . .
Rik is wielding a 'Mini-Taser' device and Johnny has on a set of brass knuckles. . .

Raji hears something. . . he stops and listens. Footsteps stop, a few steps after his. He turns and looks behind. Rik and Johnny have ducked into an alcove, and are out of sight. . .

Raji continues on and comes to a sharp turn in the hallway. Rik and Johnny pick up their pace and are ready to pounce. . .
But when they turn the corner, they see Raji talking with Ron Givens. . .
They put on their 'brakes', but still nearly collide with Raji and Ron, as Ron reacts loudly. . .

"Hey, slow down, 'Fellas'!
How'd you get in here, so LATE?

This is a 'Restricted' Area. . ."

Rik tries to make a believable excuse. . .

"We got lost. . . I guess."

"Well, I suggest you 'turn around' and 'Exit' through the door marked, 'To Stadium Exit', right down this hall on, Your LEFT."

Ron gestures back down the hallway. . .

Johnny and Rik quickly excuse themselves. . .

"Uh. . . Thanks, Boss. . . We'll do just that. . ."

Rik and Johnny slowly turn around, glancing back at Raji a few times. . .

"Hmm. . . that was weird, Raji."

TIME JUMP: It's almost Two AM by the time Raji and Ron start walking back across the almost pitch-black Playing Field, to check out the other Team's Dugouts and Locker Rooms. . .

Ron is first to remark. . .

"They're 'Nowhere', around here, Raji."

"But they're Here, Ron. The Cops, said so. They have 'No Video', of them leaving. . ."

"Raji, the Cops can't find them, and neither can we. . . Let's start out again. . . bright and early, tomorrow morning. . ."

"You mean leave them. . . my Mom and Sister. . . wherever they are. . . 'Over Night."

"I don't know what else we can do, Raji. . . I'll drive you, to your Apartment. . ."

"Uh. . . that's okay, Ron. . . Fazal waits for me outside. . ."

"Okay, then. . . but, get some sleep tonight, will You. . .so you'll be fresh, for the LA Game Trip?"

Ron pats Raji gently on his back. Raji watches, as Ron walks off the field, down into the tunnel heading for the Team Exit Gate. . .

Unrealized, 'Wise Guys' Rik and Johnny are hiding in the shadows of the LA Dugout, waiting.

Rik whispers to Johnny. . .

"His pal is leaving. . . Now's our chance. . ."

Raji looks all around.
Rik and Johnny slink down, then launch their run across the open Playing Field, right towards Raji, wielding their weapons to injure him!

Raji unaware of this threat, thinks to himself. . .

"Where could they be?"

When, out of nowhere, KESH answers him, in a 'Booming', Very Powerful 'Voice'. . .

"Where they are 'Safe and Sound', under my complete. . . CONTROL!"

Raji is instantly startled. His head jerks toward the 'Sound of the Voice'. . .

"Who's, THERE?"

The 'Wise Guys' Rik and Johnny 'STOP DEAD' in their tracks, startled, looking all around for the source of the 'Booming Voice'.

KESH then gestures with his arms, causing ALL the Lights to explode 'ON' sequentially, around the Entire Stadium. . .
'Blasting' everyone's eyes, with intense 'Sunlight' blinding illumination. . .
KESH himself, transforms into 'The Evil Hindu God KALI's' persona.
He is 'Seven Feet Tall' with flashing 'Neon Red Eyes'. . .

Rik whispers nervously, to Johnny. . .

"Who the hell is that?!"

Johnny jokes, his answer. . .

"Their. . . Mascot?"

Rik responds. . .

"No, stupid. . . there's some 'very weird' stuff goin' on around here. . ."

Raji is wide-eyed and terrified, as he looks upon the 'Evil Hindu God'. . . KALI. . .

"I know YOU. . . You are the 'Nemesis' of 'The Hindu God Hanuman'. . . you're 'KALI'."

"Nice to be recognized, by a MORTAL 'non-believer' like you Raji."

"I've BEEN CONVERTED NOW, KALI. . ."

Across the Field hiding, Johnny again, murmurs softly to Rik. . .

"It's. . . He's. . . That's a freakin. . .
. . . 'HINDU, GAWD'!"

As KALI, Kesh has become physically much larger and much more powerful. He draws his 'Large Sabre' and walks slowly toward Raji. . .

Suddenly TERRIFIED. . . Rik and Johnny look at one another in fear. . .

"That freakin' 'GAWD's got, a freakin' Giant Sword!"

KALI is carrying the 'Old Leather Cricket Ball'. . .
Raji's 'Talisman', which 'Glows' slightly in 'Neon
Blue' tones. . .
He tosses it up and down several times, then
juggles it. . .then HOLDS it. . .as Raji calls him
out loudly. . .

"You. . . You're the ONE. . . You Stole my 'Ball'!"

KESH screams back, more violently at Raji. . .

"Correction, 'MORTAL'. . .
. . . I now have. . . 'MY BALL'. . ."

Suddenly, from the 'A's Bullpen'. . .
. . . 'The Peanut Vendor' walks onto the field. . .

Raji sees the poor Mortal entering the Playing
Field and shouts to him. . .

"Sir, please take cover. You are in lethal danger!"

'Without Warning', The Vendor's Eyes flash
'Neon Blue' and his vendor's uniform transforms
into 'The Hindu God Hanuman's Golden
Bejeweled Robe'. . .

His size also reaches over Seven Feet and His
Power increases, right before Raji's eyes.
Hanuman, then draws his 'Golden Sabre'.

Raji screams jubilantly. . .

"My Great God Hanuman. . .Welcome to my Stadium!"

KALI then, calls out sarcastically. . .

HANUMAN! . . . I am honored by your presence!

In a 'FLASH', Master Kahmal also emerges onto the Playing Field. . .
From the well of the A's Dugout. . . He is wielding a 'Magical Sword', as well. . .

Shocked. . . Johnny grabs Rik. . .

"Jesus, Mother Mary! Two more GAWDS!"

"With 'Swords', Johnny. . . Let's get the 'Hell' outta here. . .

"Yeah. . . Who cares who wins this freakin' Series. . . Even if, Rob and Gino wanna kill us."

"I'd rather be killed by them. than these freakin' Giant GAWDS, Johnny!"

'Out of the Blue', Rik and Johnny turn and run for the nearest Exit Gate, never to be seen again.

Raji watches the two Men from the Inner Hallway, scatter across the Playing Field and Exit through the Player's Gate, then turns to his 'Old Coach, Major Kahmal'. . . calling his name. . .

"Master Kahmal!"

KALI also sees him and seethes his name. . .

"So we also, meet again, KAHMAL. . . Ready to lose, YOUR OTHER ARM?"

"I'm ready to take 'ONE OF YOURS, KALI', to replace my missing ONE."

In lightning speed, a sword fight between KALI, HANUMAN and KAHMAL ensues. . .
The fight is brutal and vicious.
The clanging of the Swords and Sabres are deafening. . .
The slashes and strikes of the weapons, literally electrify the air throughout the Stadium. . .

Raji stands back, helpless, as ONLY A MORTAL, in the 'Vicious Battle of Giants', that seems unending. . .
When the 'Battle' seems like a hopeless stand-off, KALI throws the 'Leather Ball' like a 'Rocket' at the feet of HANUMAN, causing him to lose his balance and slam onto the ground. . .
He hits his head hard and passes out. . .

KALI then attacks KAHMAL, with his powerful Sabre causing KAHMAL, to stumble backwards and also fall. . .
HANUMAN is coming to, but KALI kicks his 'Golden Sabre' away from his reach. . .

KALI's Sabre is about to come down on
KAHMAL's remaining arm. . .

Raji is in PANIC. . .

A short distance away, by the 'A's Bullpen',
He spies a 'Wire Basket' Filled with Baseballs.
Out of instinct, he rushes over to the 'Basket',
picks up a 'Ball' and Fires it, like a 'Mortar Shell'
at KALI. . .

Instantly, KALI gasps, as the incredibly 'Fast
Hard Ball' hits him in the torso knocking the
wind out of him. . .
But KALI regroups and recovers with a 'Vile
Vengeance'. . . now. he comes at Raji. . .
Raji picks up another 'Ball', aims it and to his
surprise, 'The Neon Blue Color' returns to his
brain's EYE, covering everything, but 'KALI's
Head'. . .
Raji fires the 'Ball'. . .
It nearly rips KALI's Ear off.

KALI is clearly weakened, but Raji is relentless.
He picks up 'Ball', after 'Ball', after 'Ball' in rapid
succession, aims, then fires a 'Barrage of Rocket-
Fueled Baseballs' at KALI. . .
Finally toppling, The Evil 'GOD KALI'. . .

HANUMAN and KAHMAL recover, then grab
their own 'Golden Sabre' and Sword, advancing
toward the wounded KALI. . .

KALI, badly injured, and unable to continue the fight, fades into a ghostly 'Neon Red' Vapor.

But in one last desperate act, he brings his 'Sabre' down on the 'Old Leather Cricket Ball'. . . It explodes in flames, and is 'Destroyed'. . .

HANUMAN looks to Raji, grateful for his help. . .

"You saved me, once again, Young Man . . ."

MAJOR KAHMAL, also acknowledges Raji. . .

"And me, as well, my Young Protégé. . .And in the process, You, have rediscovered your POWER!

"But it is gone again, Master. KALI destroyed 'The Old Leather Ball'. . .it went up in flames. . ."

HANUMAN looks deeply into Raji's eyes. . .

"Raji, 'Your Power' was NEVER in 'The Talisman,' in that 'Old Yellow Ball'. . .

It was always in your heart and deep in your 'Soul' all along. . .
You NEVER lost it. . . you just convinced yourself that you had, but that was your 'Mind' telling your 'Heart', Lies. . .
Your 'Soul' always had it. . .
Always had the 'Ball Power'. . ."

BOTH, God and Super-Mortal softly add. . .

"We must go now, Raji, pleased to know your 'Soul' will have the 'FULL'. . . 'Blue Neon Power of the Gods', forever!"

The GOD HANUMAN and KAHMAL begin to fade into ghostly forms, walking across the Playing Field off into the 'Dreamworld', together. . .

Desperately, Raji pleads to their disappearing images. . .

"But My Mother and My Sister. . .Where. . ."

KAHMAL's fading voice answers. . .

"They are fine, Raji. . ."

The GOD HANUMAN turns back towards Raji. . . As his voice, also begins trailing off. . .

"Look for 'My Peanut Vendor's Cart'. It will take you to them."

In the next instant, 'Both' Ghostly Images become, 'Hallowed Ether'. . .
As Tears, begin stinging, Raji's eyes. . .

TIME JUMP: The Night is drawing to a close and the dawn clouds are breaking over the Mountains to the East of the Stadium. . .

Raji walks cautiously down a darkened interior Stadium hallway. . . looking everywhere. . .

After turning a corner, he sees a 'Vendor's Cart', a short distance ahead.

He approaches the 'Magical Cart' cautiously, then looks all around it, slowly grasping the handle. . .

The 'Cart' takes off at breakneck speeds, as Raji sprints along behind it. . .
Then suddenly, it stops, at a brick wall. . .
His shoulders slump. . .

Raji thinks, to himself, about what to do next. . .

'Wonderful! The cart has taken me to a brick wall.'

Raji sighs and starts to walk away. . .
But 'Magically', the bricks begin to drop off the wall, one by one, revealing a doorway. . .

Raji's eyes are wide with anticipation. He furiously tosses more bricks aside himself and throws open the door. . .

To his delight and to theirs, Veena and Khaldoon emerge from the room. Hugs, kisses and tears all around. . .

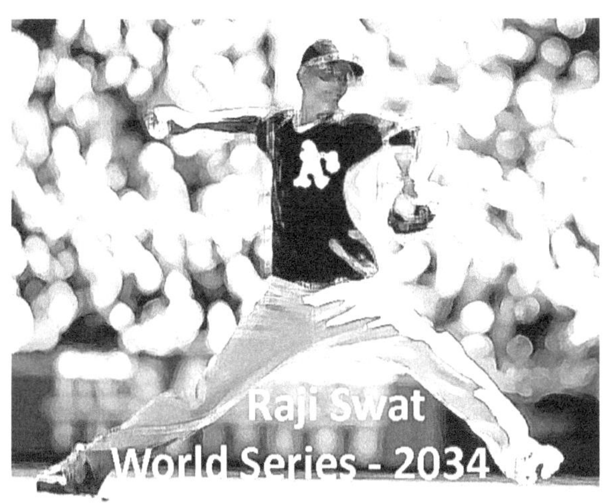

Chapter 20

The Final Strike

COSCO STADIUM - OAKLAND, CALIFORNIA:

TIME JUMP: It's Four, in the afternoon, back in Oakland, for the Final Games of the Series, at the massive COSCO Stadium.

The Oakland A's have now made a Three Game 'Streak Comeback' in Los Angeles, with Raji's Relief Pitching. . .

This is the First Game back at their 'COSCO Stadium Home Field' and it's the 'Top of the Ninth Inning'. . . LA Dodger's at Bat. . .with Two Outs. . .

2034 World Series

GAME Score: LA Dodgers - 2- Games
Oakland A's - 3- Games

Today's Scoreboard: Dodgers - 6 : A's - 7

Raji Swat is standing on the Mound. He winds up, aims and fires a 'Rocket'. The Dodger batter swings and misses by a mile.

Broadcast Booth: Announcer, Rhodes. . .

"He scattered the pigeons on that one!"

Ames adds his color update. . .

"Dodgers are now down, Two Outs . . .thanks to Raji. . . If he Strikes this Guy Out. . . The Series is Over and Oakland Wins it, without another Game. . .First Time in Forty Years!"

Pitcher's Mound: Raji does his wind-up and focuses on Sammy's Catcher's Mitt. . . everything else is blocked from his view.

He throws a ball that seems to 'STOP' in midair, slow down, curve downward and then speed up. Marcus, the Dodger's Batter Swings and Misses.

Broadcast Booth: Rhodes calls it. . .

"You see that?! Zipped right through his wheelhouse!"

Ames fills in the banter. . .

"Nope. . . and neither did Marcus!"

They share a laugh, as Ames makes the last call.

"One more 'Strike' and the World Series belongs to the Oakland A's. . .and Raji Swat. . .

Pitcher's Mound: Raji goes through his ritual. He winds up, focuses on the target spot, throws and Strikes Marcus out. . . Game, Series, and Season Over. . .

Broadcast Booth: Rhodes yelling. . .

"Go crazy, Folks, Go crazy!"

Ames laughs. . .

"Finally, I can die and go to 'Heaven Now'!"

The stadium is in chaos. . . jubilant A's fans are in 'Ecstasy'. . . Dodger fans are disappointed, but even they, join in the chanting. . .

"Ra-ji! Ra-ji! Raji MVP! . . ."
"Ra-ji! Ra-ji! Raji MVP!"

The A's Players, Duke and Jake all surround Raji Swat, then hoist him up on their shoulders, as the 'Hero' of the World Series '2034'.

END STORY FLASHBACK:

"It was truly the highlight of my Career at Oakland that day, in 2034, when my 'Teammates', finally accepted me.

I also won 'World Series MVP' and a 'Tickertape Parade' in Downtown Oakland, where I was in the Lead Car. . .

The street was lined with avid fans cheering me on. Plus, riding in the Car with me, was a jubilant Ron Givens and Fazal."

RAJI'S MANSION - Private island - Indian Ocean

The palm trees surrounding the mansion sway gently in the night breeze. Soft lighting washes down the mansion walls, highlighting it against the dark night.

Interior Dining Room, Raji is seated in the chic surroundings, addressing the camera.

"So that is 'My Story', or most of the 'high and low' points. . .

With the support of the entire team, Coach "promoted" me to 'Starting Pitcher' for the 'Next Season', with a nice raise.

For me, it's never been about the money, although, it continues to rain down on me.

We went on to win the World Series the next Three Years, which was last year, 2037. We hope to win again in the upcoming season 2038."

A maid serves Raji, a plate of food. . .

He picks up his fork, but then stops and looks at the camera again.

"Oh, one last thing. Remember when I found my Mother and my Sister?

Kahmal and Hanuman were right. . . I also found myself and everything I thought I had lost."

Raji smiles, his typical charming grin. . .

"There was one more 'Captive' who emerged from that 'Hidden Room' in the Stadium that Night."

Raji looks off camera at a beautiful Indian girl, who walks into the room and returns Raji's smile, with the same intensity as his. . .

It's Lalita, his lost Love.

Raji gazes at her with a twinkle in his eye.

"I may be isolated. . . but I'm not alone. . ."

Lalita sits down at the table, next to Raji.

She gives him a little kiss. . .

They laugh and talk. Then, they both dig into their incredible dinner. . .

THE END

*This Fantasy Novel,
'The Cricketer'
is Dedicated
to my Two, Young, 'Baseball Loving', Grandsons,
Brandon (an Excellent Lefty Pitcher)
and
Mack (an Excellent Right-Handed Catcher)*